Beyond Religion

Creating Intimacy with The Most High

Candace L. Campbell

DYNASTY LIFE
Publishing

Scripture quotations taken from the following translations:

King James Version (KJV). Public domain.

New King James Version (NKJV). Scripture taken from the New King James Version®. Copyright © 1982 by Thomas Nelson. Used by permission. All rights reserved.

Names of God Bible (NOG). The Names of God Bible (without notes). © 2011 by Baker Publishing Group.

Complete Jewish Bible (CJB). Copyright © 1998 by David H. Stern. All rights reserved.

New International Version (NIV). Holy Bible, New International Version®, NIV®. Copyright © 1973, 1978, 1984, 2011 by Biblica, Inc.® Used by permission. All rights reserved worldwide.

First Edition

Note on Cepher Bible:

Cepher Hardback - Cepher Millennial Edition.
Cepher Mobile Version - 22.0.48.

Cover Design by Dario Delos

ISBN 979-8-9945514-0-0 (Paperback)
ISBN 979-8-9945514-1-7 (eBook)
ISBN 979-8-9945514-2-4 (Hardback)
Published by Dynasty Life Publishing

For permissions or inquiries, contact: Beyondreligion@dynastylife.net

Contents

Introduction

The inspiration for this book is an ongoing spiritual transition that began about 7 years ago from the time of this writing. Although I had been a self-professing Christian for almost all of my life, it was during a very dark period in 2017 that I had the "born again" experience that left me permanently transformed. This did not take place within the walls of a church but rather on the floor of my room at my mama's house. Being at my lowest point, I cried out to my Heavenly Father in true repentance, apologizing for "ruining" and wasting the life He gave me. I promised that if He would help me, I would do whatever He said.

Afterwards, I fasted for a few days. When it was over, something in me had changed. It was as if a veil had been lifted off my eyes. I saw the Most High, the Scriptures, and the world completely differently.

Growing up in church it was often said that we needed to have a personal relationship with Jesus but I don't believe I fully grasped what that meant. Aside from someone occasionally *catching* the Holy Spirit, there was not much talk of spirituality or prophetic gifting. This would all change soon as about a year and a half following my transformation, I found myself back in Los Angeles where I was led to join a brand-new church in Santa Monica. New, as in, the first day I visited was the day they opened. Where I'm from, churches seemed to have always been there, so I was intrigued to find out what it was like for a church to just *start* out of nowhere.

This new church considered itself moderately charismatic and proved to be a safe place for me to go deeper in communicating with the Holy Spirit. When it came to hearing from the Most High, He used our small, close-knit group of Believers to sharpen my spiritual discernment. Up to this point, I had prayed regularly over the course of my life, read the Bible several times over, and fasted on many occasions. What was missing was that I didn't know how to hear from Yah with intentionality. Yes, He had led me over the years and there had been certain signs, but I wasn't aware that I could engage Him in a two-way discussion and that it was much easier than I had imagined.

As I write this, 1 Thessalonians 5:17 comes to mind where we are instructed to pray without ceasing. For many of us, this seems like a daunting task when operating under the assumption that it's on us to carry most of the conversation. In my faith tradition, it had been implied, if not outright taught, that God only spoke to us through His Word. I had indeed experienced instances of this, however, through this church and the listening prayer para-ministry that they were associated with, I learned how to quiet myself to hear from Yah and discern my own voice from His (and others). I also began to experience the lovely gift of confirmation, both through my own encounters as well as through fellow Believers. I discovered that I could hear from Yah directly through my own thoughts, through others, nature and countless other channels. I speak of this more in-depth in the book as I will detail a defining moment where I reached a pinnacle point in my faith where there was no turning back.

In the Spring of 2020 the lockdowns began and I was consequently laid off from my job. I also knew, intuitively, that the world would never be the same again. I sensed that the Most High wanted me to go even deeper in Him. I wasn't quite sure what that meant but I felt very strongly in my spirit that I needed to make myself available to whatever it was that He was calling me to. The only problem was that my current church kept me very busy.

I had joined the prayer team, was co-leading a small group and supporting other church functions. Community was one of our top priorities, so we also spent a significant amount of time just hanging out with one another. As much as I cared for them, I knew that I had to make room for the new thing that the Most High wanted to do in my life. Again, I didn't fully know what all that would entail. I just knew I had to shake off anything that would serve as a distraction to that prompting.

By April, I had given up my leadership position and left the church. I still fellowshipped with other Believers, attended Bible study via Zoom, and like everyone else, I watched church online enjoying the freedom of receiving from several ministers that taught on a variety of topics.

That summer proved to be life changing and it was confirmed that I'd made the right decision. I was released from the stronghold of a relationship that I had been trying to get free from for over 3 years. The accompanying low-level depression that it caused was lifted as well.

I also sensed that this was *thee* opportunity for me to make the transition out of corporate America which I had been attempting, unsuccessfully, for almost four years. With unemployment and stimulus checks to support this endeavor, I knew it was now or never to make the move into entrepreneurship.

Amid all of this, a good friend of mine started a Black Women's Writer Group. We were all at varying degrees of our career with me being pretty close to the bottom. Some women had almost finished projects, others were on the verge of publishing, and my accountability partner was already a TV writer for a major show.

Suddenly, after 12 years, the way of Hollywood had finally made its way to my universe and I realized that the old *who you know* game could catapult me into a land of opportunities that I previously hadn't thought possible.

The reality that I needed to gain clarity on exactly what I wanted to do with my life was becoming crystal clear. At this stage in the game, the last thing I needed was to end up with a good thing that wasn't a Yah thing. This wasn't just limited to my writing career. Now that the world was seemingly at my fingertips, I asked myself, *"what are the actual things that you want out of life across the board?"* This led me to sit with the Holy Spirit and come up with 8 different objectives that included career, family life, ministry, etc.

That August, the ministry that I was following at the time was teaching on Rosh Hashanah. (In fact, over the years many seeds were planted that steered towards the Hebraic roots of my faith.) Of course, I'd heard of it before but for some reason, this time, as the minister explained the difference between the Gregorian calendar and the Hebrew one (Yah's Calendar), it resonated with me. With my newfound understanding, I actually became a little indignant. Like yeah, who is *man* to change when the year is going to start? If the Lord says that it's the New Year in September, then so be it! I was feeling like a new woman in need of a reset anyway, so my sentiment was immediately, *let's do this!* I've since come to understand that the physical Hebraic New Year actually starts in Spring, but I was at least headed in the right direction!

In preparation, the ministry leader called for an 8-day corporate fast as we learned about the Hebrew letter Chet. I thought to myself, what a coincidence! I can take my 8 objectives and put one before the Lord for each day of the fast to get more direction!

The results of that fast were life changing. I experienced a time of unprecedented spiritual breakthrough and Yah answered me in detail on every single one of our objectives. It was an intense time, and His downloads kept coming even days after the fast ended. I can only liken it to being at an amusement park all day, into the night, and being completely worn out but still not wanting to leave because I was enjoying myself so much. I recall repeatedly telling Yah that this is too much (in the best of ways). I was also clear that I didn't want it to stop until I received everything He had for me. Little did I know, I was just getting started. Five years later I continue to see things being fulfilled from that time with still more to come.

If I were to chronicle everything that happened from then until now, this introduction would turn into the book itself. However, there was one particular point that I do want to detail. In January of 2021, I was attending an online School of the Prophets from a minister that I'd been following for some time. To be clear, I wasn't attending because I thought I was a prophet, but I knew I had some type of prophetic gifting, as anyone with the Holy Spirit does, and I wanted to gain a deeper understanding of it. Some of my cohorts were, indeed, prophets, or at least *extremely* prophetic. They were the real deal. I had never met these folks a day in my life, but they were telling me things about myself that I knew only the Most High would have revealed to them.

There was one specific thing spoken to me by a particular woman that I consider a significant marker in my spiritual journey. She said that she saw me "expanding outside the four walls of the church." By then, I had relocated to a different state, and we were still much into the throws of the pandemic. As a result, or so I thought, I was still not a member of a church. In my mind, it was a temporary situation that I was sure would resolve itself once the dust settled. I interpreted her prophecy to mean that I would one day be a member of a church but that my ministry would expand beyond it. With that in mind, and spirit, when Yah transitioned me to the next place, which I sensed was a more permanent situation, I began to seek out a church home. After, several ironically poor experiences later, I realized that wasn't it. I'd experienced yet another major spiritual awakening since leaving L.A. and all the pieces were beginning to come together.

Even so, for someone who had spent most of her life in church, it was a disorienting place to be, and truthfully, I didn't know what to do with myself. So, I leaned into what had sustained me over the past couple of years: worshiping, praying, listening, reading, and journaling. I knew enough to trust that I couldn't go wrong with those practices.

Within a couple of months of my last attempt to attend a church gathering, the Most High supernaturally began to connect me with like-minded Believers. It was obvious that these individuals were sent to water the seeds that had been planted for several years as they helped me grow beyond everything I thought I knew. To be clear, I will never grow beyond the Father, His Word both written and in the Person of the Messiah, or the Holy Spirit. They are and will remain the foundation of my faith. However, the Most High has given me so much revelation as to how far present-day Believers have gotten from the Truth. We have been so steeped in deception that we are unable to discern between Christianity and The Way as prescribed by the Scripture.

Beyond Religion: Creating Intimacy with The Most High is not about bashing religion. There are many edifying principles that we established through the vessel of religious constructs. They have provided a structure for Believers to learn and implement spiritual disciplines to support us as the foundation of our faith is being built. The purpose of this book is to show how to have a tangible engaging relationship with the Elohiym of Abraham, Isaac, and Jacob.

I wrote **Beyond Religion** because I am not special in the sense that the same relationship that I possess with the Father is available to anyone who diligently seeks Him. One of my greatest heart's desires is for others to experience Him in a way that transforms their mind, body, and spirit beyond what they could have ever imagined. It is an invitation to be completely free, whole, and lacking nothing. It is the living thread of my testimony in motion: fluid, sacred and still unfolding.

Journey with me through these pages, where wisdom meets testimony, peppered with my own firsthand experiences that will encourage you on the path that has been crafted exclusively for you, as the son or daughter of The Most High, King of Glory.

Preface

How To Read Beyond Religion

The introduction to **Beyond Religion** includes my statement of faith and an overview of my personal testimony. The Word tells us to know those who labor among us, and so I believe it's important for readers to have an understanding of my core beliefs and some insight into who I am.

Beyond Religion can be read individually or as part of a small group. I would suggest having a Bible on hand to look up the Scriptures referenced in the book. Sometimes the full Scripture will be written out, and other times only book, chapter, and verse will be given to support a principle or paraphrase. If you have trouble reading the Word, this book will give you ample opportunity to change that. Take your time and look up the Scriptures cited in the footnotes.

Next is the matter of language. The premise of this book is truth, as you cannot have a relationship with the Creator without it. The Messiah speaks of this in John 4:23 when He says, "But the hour cometh, and now is, when the true worshippers shall worship the Father in spirit and in truth: for the Father seeketh such to worship Him."

The hour is here, and the truth is that the Word was given to the Hebrew people, and from beginning to end, it is a redemptive story about the Hebrew people through the sacrifice of a Hebrew Messiah. For proper context and to get the most out of Scripture, we must be intentional about understanding the Hebraic culture and language.

With that said, throughout Scripture, the Creator speaks at length about His name; from instructing His people to call upon His name to even calling His people by His name. We know that "God" is a title and not a name. We also know that the Scriptures say there are many gods. Finally, we know that there is *power* in His name. I believe that the modern-day trend to call the Creator by a generic title is intentional, and if you have eyes to see, the enemy has exposed his hand in this crafty device.

In resistance to the demonic/Babylonian influence which has transformed the faith of our Hebrew ancestors into something many of them would hardly recognize today, I have embraced Hebraic names of the Father and the Son and will be using them in this writing.

Keeping in mind that these names may be unfamiliar to some, please find brief explanations below.

Name	Transliteration	Meaning	Scripture Reference
Yahuah	The Father	Existing One, I AM, I was, I will be.	Exodus 3:13-15
Yahusha	The Son/Messiah	I AM He who saves, delivers, rescues. I AM salvation.	Matthew 1:21 Acts 4:12
The Most High	The Most High	Above all, including other gods.	Psalms 97:9
Yah	Short for Yahuah	I AM	Psalm 68:4
Elohiym	God	The Creator	Genesis 1:1

I also often refer to the Creator as the Most High or use Yah for short. There are also times when it seems appropriate to use "Elohiym", which is the Hebraic word for God.

Again, it is important to know that truth matters, and that Truth is a person (John 14:6). While there may be some discrepancies regarding the pronunciation and spelling of the Hebraic names, we can be certain that the Father's name is not "God," nor was the Messiah a Greek man. Therefore, He was not given a Greek name. So, in obedience to the leading of the Holy Spirit and allegiance to the Truth, in Beyond Religion, I will use the Hebraic names as my current understanding dictates.

Finally, and most importantly, I would plead with anyone reading this book to pray and ask for the Holy Spirit to give you understanding, insight, and revelation as you read. This will help you to keep an open mind to things you may not have heard or considered before. It will also allow you to think critically from a place of safety rather than being limited by fear since this may cause you to question some things you were previously taught.

Be honest with yourself about what hasn't made sense and have the courage to ask the Holy Spirit to make things clearer for you. Even if you've never prayed a prayer like that before, give the Most High the opportunity to confirm that He is indeed speaking to you through this writing. After all, communicating with Him is essentially what this book is about so let's begin there. The Holy Spirit will never mislead you. Therefore, it's imperative that you request His presence while reading this book.

PART I

Religion vs Relationship

CHAPTER 1

Understanding Religion

Growing up, when I thought of the word religion, I assumed it meant adhering to the overall themes of the Christian faith. As for those who did not subscribe to the teachings of the Bible, I considered them to be in a false religion. Over the years, my experiences have led me to take a deeper look into the construct of religion as a whole. Let us begin with the following online definition provided by a reputable reference publisher:

Religion

1:   a personal set or institutionalized system of religious attitudes, beliefs, and practices

2:   a (1): the service and worship of God or the supernatural
(2): commitment or devotion to religious faith or observance
b: the state of a religious [sic]

3:   a cause, principle, or system of beliefs held to with ardor and faith

4:   archaic : scrupulous conformity : CONSCIENTIOUSNESS

Interestingly enough, the primary definition makes no mention of God at all. The first half of it centers the individual as it proudly defines religion as personal. This means that it can vary from person to person. The latter half states that religion is an institutionalized system of religious attitudes, beliefs, and practices. We would find similar attributes if we looked up the definition of culture, which like personal beliefs, are subject to change. This is especially true today, since by way of technology, our global society allows cultures to influence one another on a much grander scale than what we've seen in recent history.

When we examine the religion of modern-day Christianity it is not hard to see how culture has influenced the faith rather than the other way around. On the surface, mainstream Christianity has the vital components of the overarching redemptive story but oftentimes the way that it is presented is still to the benefit of man. What makes *man* feel comfortable and secure? What keeps *man* filled with hope for a prosperous life on Earth? What makes *man* feel content with identities they've assumed which are contrary to the Creator's design, and so on.

The subjective nature of many teachings gives man the freedom to reshape the Elohiym of Scripture into a god made in his own image. This is where phrases like "My God wouldn't do that" begin to surface, which reflect personal preference instead of truth. At times, we even dare to sit in judgment of Him, saying things like, "If He were truly loving, He would do this…", or "He wouldn't allow that." It's as if we have decided for ourselves who Yahuah is rather than learning and accepting who *He* says He is according to how He has revealed Himself through Scripture. Instead of relying on offhand remarks and selectively pulled verses that validate our opinions, we should be using the whole of Scripture to obtain an accurate and robust understanding of the Father.

In this generation, both individual and cultural preferences are elevated above the Word. The result is a faith that is highly destabilized. Within it, ideals are always shifting and the lines between good and evil are blurred. This is the reason for so many divisions and denominations. It also attributes to the fact that there is often little distinction between so-called Believers and non-Believers. If the Word was truly our anchor, we would be on one accord and easily identifiable as different. The Creator says that His people are peculiar.[1]

What is often referred to as religion is *culture* mixed with key Bible verses that may or may not be misinterpreted. This in turn gives birth to a religious system rather than an actual Biblical way of living. To be clear, Yahusha never commanded His followers to be a part of any system. Early Believers that were a part of the renewed covenant referred to themselves as followers of The Way which is the Messiah.[2] In fact, when Scripture references the "world", we would be wise to include the world systems as part of that. 2 Corinthians 4:4 plainly says that satan is the god of this world and it is clear that a demonic agenda has infiltrated every aspect of our societal infrastructure.

The enemy plays the long game, planting seemingly harmless seeds hundreds and thousands of years in advance that, once mature, are ripe with wickedness. Some would argue that these systems have not merely been taken over by the enemy but were actually satanic in origin. This makes sense when we know that his ultimate plan is to bring humankind under subjection to the beast system.[3] This systematic oppression is not exclusive to Christianity but encompasses all world religions and stretches across the major mountains of influence including the educational system, the healthcare system, the justice system, etc.

---

[1] 1 Peter 2:9
[2] Acts 24:14, John 14:6
[3] Revelation 13:16-17

The Way vs Christianity

While these observations may not be new to Believers with a discerning eye, I would suspect that many would find these claims to be jarring. The revelation lies within understanding the nature of Elohiym and contrasting it with that of man, specifically as it relates to change.

Yahuah, Himself says that He does not change[4] and the Scripture also states that Yahusha is the same, today, yesterday and forever[5]. In 1 Samuel 15:29 a sharp contrast is made between the nature of Yah and that of humanity. It calls out man as the one who changes his mind. If we're honest, we see this everyday as mans' perspective is constantly shifting according to his own convenience, benefit, and desire. We are the ultimate hypocrites and it's not limited to religion. It is the very nature of carnal man to make rules and exceptions according to what we believe to be right. Therefore, based on the authority of Scripture and what we know to be true about human behavior, we can conclude that any *changes* to how we have been instructed to worship the Creator, or relate to one another, has been initiated by man.

How exactly has man changed things? To answer this, we must understand what actual Biblical living entails. We do that by looking at the example given in the person of Yahusha Ha'Mashiach who came to fulfill, not do away with, the law also known as Torah. Modern Believers err when they reduce Torah to The Law of Moses. To be clear, the law was given to Moses by Yah, as a means of His instruction, desire and will for the governance of His people. It is His Word. Yahusha is the Word made flesh. The Messiah could

---

[4] Malachi 3:6
[5] Hebrews 13:8

fulfill the Word because He was/is the Word. First century Believers understood this and embodied Revelation 14:12 which speaks of the saints that keep the commandments of Elohiym and the faith of Yahusha. So, what does it mean to keep the commandments of Elohiym? Again, it goes back to Torah which refers to the law given to Moses which entails the first five books of the Bible.

Before expounding on this next topic, I want to clarify that we do not keep Torah as a way to earn salvation but rather as a result of. Torah is about learning the foundational ways of the Father and what is pleasing to Him. Secondly, we know that Yahusha is our Passover Lamb and has given Himself as the ultimate sacrifice to remove the penalty of sin which is death. We trust and believe in that. Yet, salvation exists within the midst of the two as you cannot have one without the other.

Although the false doctrine known as "sola fide" which says that we are "saved by faith alone" is perpetuated, we see that it is in direct contrast to James 2:24 which says, "a man is justified by works, and not by faith only." The true meaning of the Scripture is akin to the Christian saying, "we do not obey God to be saved, we obey God *because* we are saved." It's the same concept. Our obedience is the proof of our ongoing salvation. The word "ongoing" is used because we *have been* saved, *are being* saved, and *will be* saved. Salvation is multifaceted. It involves ongoing renewal and a continual drawing near to perfection, shaping us into the very person the Father envisioned before He formed us in our mother's womb.[6] This is why Philippians 2:12 instructs us to **"work out our soul salvation"**. It takes more than simply believing that Yahusha died for our sins. Our

---

[6] Jeremiah 1:5

actions must be aligned with that belief for our Heavenly Father to consider it to be *saving faith.*

Unfortunately, Torah is taboo for many Believers. Some confuse it with legalism/work-based salvation while others find the whole thing to be an overwhelming impossible feat. These are all lies that the enemy has perpetuated to keep distance between us and the Father. It is the same game plan as in the days of Eden when the serpent convinced Adam and Eve to disobey Yah's commands. Torah is our guideline for living as a set-apart people, whether you are natural Israel or grafted in. Gentile Believers do not get to come into a faith and remix it with their own culture and beliefs. The culture of Messianic Believers is still deeply rooted in Torah.

Without Torah, we are left with a dangerous ambiguity: what is sin?[7] Without the Ten Commandments, which are a part of Torah, how do we know what sin is? Without the remainder of the laws, statues, and commandments, how do we know that it is wrong to have sexual relations with a close family member or an animal? Where does it say that we get to keep the things we already do not agree with such as homosexuality, while disregarding the command about consuming unclean foods, when Yahuah calls both an abomination? (Leviticus 18:22, Deuteronomy 14:3-10). Did the Father change His mind? Did the nature of a pig change?

Nowhere in Scripture does the death and resurrection of the Messiah grant us permission to live according to our own desires. In fact, the opposite is true. Let's turn to Matthew 5:17-19 to hear the Messiah's own words concerning the continued relevance of the Torah:

---

[7] 1 John 3:4

"Don't think that I have come to abolish the Torah or the Prophets. I have come not to abolish, but to complete. Yes indeed! I tell you that until heaven and earth pass away, not so much as a yud or a stroke will pass from the Torah—no until everything that must happen has happened. So whoever disobeys the least of these commandments and teaches others to do so will be called the least in the Kingdom of Heaven. But whoever obeys them and so teaches will be called great in the Kingdom of Heaven."

These are the words of Emmanuel, Elohiym with us.[8] On one hand you have modern Christianity that says that the law is done away with and we no longer have to follow it. On the other, you have The Way saying that He did not come to abolish the law and not a jot or a tittle will pass until all is fulfilled. This is the epitome of religion vs Biblical. It is a result of high-level indoctrination that tells us how to interpret Scripture instead of taking heed to the actual words that were written. In this specific example, it is important to notice that this is not Moses, John, or even Paul giving their interpretation on Torah. This is The Messiah, the Living Word, speaking. The One who expressly says in John 5:30 that He came to do the will of the Father.

Now, pay special attention to verse 19 which dispels two false teachings at once. The first one is that the Torah is done away with. Are we to believe that Yahusha was telling his followers that they only needed to follow the Torah until his resurrection and were thereafter free to live as they pleased as long as they *loved one another?* The second myth that this Scripture dismantles is that those who fail at keeping the law will not inherit the Kingdom.

---

[8] Matthew 1:23

It does not say that. It says that they will be the least in the Kingdom. So, for those of us who are living *righteously* while disregarding the Torah, we are indeed practicing a form of self righteousness. We are living according to what we think is right, not according to what the Father defines as righteous. That is not to say that there is no overlap but that should not be the case. The Kingdom is not a democracy where we get to decide with the Most High what is good and what is evil. The enemy has done a good job at making us believe that there is a middle ground but there is not. It's either Yahuah's way or the god of this world's way.[9] Therefore, having a "religion" that is only partially aligned with the will of the Father, is false. A half truth is still a lie.

Unfortunately, this a la carte style of faith-based living, called Christianity, is what's primarily taught in today's churches. As a result, according to Matthew 5:19, many of the leaders who make it into the Kingdom will have the lowest positions. Eternity is far too long to settle for merely making it in. Those who carry an 'as long as I make it in' mindset should pause and reflect, because true love for the Most High does not aim for the bare minimum, it longs to please Him. In John 14:15 Yahusha says, **"If you love me, you will keep my commandments."** He also says **"I and My Father are one"** in John 10:30. Therefore, there is no contradiction of His commandments with Yahuah's.

If there were any distinctions made between the two, we would see that Yahusha's commandments, which are still based on Torah, hold Believers to an even higher standard. The Messiah came to deal with the inner man, commanding His followers to have a

---

[9] 2 Corinthians 4:4

change of heart rather than simply following laws, statutes, and commandments.

In fact, when we do these things apart from a heart that genuinely loves the Most High, we are operating in religion. It is possible to keep the commandments of Yah and still be wicked if our thoughts and motivations are displeasing to Him. This was the sin of the pharisees who knew the Torah thoroughly and appeared outwardly righteous but had hardened hearts. Yahusha says that whosoever is angry with his brother without a cause shall be in danger of the same judgment as that of a murderer.[10] He also equates looking at a woman lustfully with adultery.[11] Messiah came to show that we cannot hide behind our religious acts which is why He was constantly reading people's minds and exposing their true intentions. Matthew 7:21-23 is the culmination of this as it blatantly tells us that we can do all these religious acts and at the very end still hear *"I never knew you; depart from me..."*

To truly know the Messiah (and by extension the Father), beyond carnal knowledge, we must be born from above or *born again* as it is said in Christianity. This happens when we have a renewed heart that not only wants to do the will of the Father but also deeply desires the Father, Himself. I'm speaking of a relationship with the Creator that goes beyond just getting our needs met. One that evolves from the self-centeredness that is both overtly and subtly encouraged in modern Christianity to a true Elohiym centered lifestyle. The carnal heart resists this truth, unable to comprehend how one could find true fulfillment in full submission to the Father's will. At its core, it's a matter of trust; one that the

---

[10] Matthew 5:21-22
[11] Matthew 5:27-28

enemy fiercely works to undermine, keeping us bound in fear and self-reliance.

This is being emphasized to explain that while Torah is vital, it alone, does not save. If it did, then there wouldn't be a need for Yahusha to offer Himself up on our behalf. We must have the change of heart that allows us to become the new creatures in Messiah that the Scriptures speak of. That change of heart also comes with the gift of the Holy Spirit who will lead us into all understanding, including the role and context of Torah.

By now, you may be wondering how and why we arrived on the topic of Torah. In this chapter, I have used it to show the difference between religion and being a true follower of Yahuah. However, understanding Torah is also a practical tip in going beyond religion and creating intimacy with the Most High. To have a relationship with someone we must know them, right? Learning Torah is how we do that.

Torah teaches us what the Father likes and what He doesn't. It also presents us with the true culture of the Kingdom. It gives us the Holy Convocations and Feast Days that honor the Father and the Son instead of holidays such as Christmas and Easter that are rooted in idolatrous pagan practices. Remember, this is a Hebraic faith in which others are grafted in. [12] Messiah clearly said that He was only sent unto the lost sheep of Israel. [13] That does not mean others are not welcome, but that they must come in humility and assimilate to the culture of the Kingdom, which is Torah. [14]

---

[12] Romans 11:17

[13] Matthew 15:24

[14] Romans 11:18

CHAPTER 2

Origins of Christianity

B *eyond Religion: Creating Intimacy with The Most High* is not about church history. The meat of this book contains practical tips on how to develop intimacy with the Most High and I promise you we will get there. However, it is difficult to experience true intimacy in any relationship without a foundation built on truth. This chapter is meant to provide enough of an overview to expose the process in which Believers were finessed from following the actual Messiah to becoming a part of a religious system loosely built on the Bible. To do this, we must begin with the source to understand when the shift began to take place.

In chapter one, we discussed how first century Believers accepted Yahusha as the One who took on the penalty of sin for all who believed. The result of this belief caused them to obey the commandments of the Messiah which are one with the Father. It is important to understand that they still followed Torah, coupled with the doctrine of the gospel. Obviously, parts of the sacrificial law were done away with because Yahusha became the ultimate sacrifice for sin.

After the death of Yahusha, His followers were largely persecuted by the Roman empire resulting in many of them fleeing to various parts of the world. Roman leaders saw an opportunity to use the Hebraic faith to their advantage in gaining dominance and control over other nations. One major way they accomplished this was by removing Israelites from leadership positions. They forbade them from practicing their faith as defined in Scripture which included prohibiting Sabbath worship and disregarding the dietary laws.

Names were also hellenized. 2 Chronicles 7:14 is often used to remind Believers about the role of humility in their times of need. Yet, the first part of that verse, ***"My people who are called by My name..."*** is glossed over. Not only does the nation of Yasharel (Israel) contain His name, but many of His people were individually named after Him. His holy name has been erased from Yahusha, Yermeyahu, Mattithyahu and replaced with Greek versions such as Joshua/Jesus, Jeremiah, and Matthew.

Additionally, the ineffable name doctrine was put into effect replacing Yahuah's name with *God* and *Lord* throughout Scripture. This left verses like Psalms 83:18 senseless. The concept of the *Old* and *New* Testament was also invented, paving the way for Torah to be considered irrelevant.

Not only were these new stipulations put into place as a hindrance to the Hebrews, but they also used the Christian religion to oppress one another. After much fighting, the European nations eventually came together to streamline the faith. This led to the formation of the Council of Nicea who instituted Easter and changed the day of worship to Sunday along with other customs still practiced by Catholic and Protestant churches to this day. Additionally, several books were removed from the ancient writings leaving what is now referred to as canon, the traditional 66 books of the Bible. As a result, it is considered unnecessary, if not dangerous, for Believers to read anything beyond it.

It's important to note that these so-called leaders were pagan converts. During their construction of Christianity, they integrated many of their pagan practices into the faith. Eventually this led to the European wars, also known as the Crusades. Ironically, none of these things had anything to do with the Israelites or the Messianic Hebraic faith. Nevertheless, after all of this funny math of adding, subtracting, and unnecessary carrying on, we were left with what is now known as Christianity.

Before we continue, we should reiterate that in Matthew 15:24, the Messiah said out of His own mouth that He only came for the lost sheep of Israel. Israel's entire purpose was to be set apart to glorify the One True Living Elohiym before all the nations. This has always been the case and did not change with the death and resurrection of Yahusha. However, as we know, due to Israel's unbelief, the Most High allowed other nations to be grafted in.[15] Yet, the order remained the same. Israel, carriers of the Torah, were now also charged with sharing the gospel of Yahusha Ha'Mashiach to all nations.

The roots of the Christian religious system are being exposed now more than ever. As inclusivity is elevated above all, we can see how the split from Catholicism and Protestantism was largely a farce, with both roads leading to the same destination: universalism. The word *catholic* means **"broad in sympathies, tastes, and interests."** When capitalized, Catholic refers to the universal church. The ritualistic nature of Catholicism, unhealthy obsession with Mary, the saints, and the level of authority given to the Pope and priests are all easily identifiable ways that differ from Protestantism. However, the preoccupation with the cross, Sunday worship, and pagan holiday observance seen in Protestant churches are all remnants of Catholicism. Again, the forefathers of this *New*

---

[15] Romans 11:11-31

Age faith were Romans and Greeks. They were not given authority to use key elements of Scripture to create their own religious system.

Believers of The Way acknowledge, but do not pedestalize, Miryam as the mother of Yahusha. We regard Messiah as the head of the called-out assembly and recognize Him as our mediator rather than a human priest. We also support that the Messiah died on a tree as a fulfillment of Scripture[16], kept Sabbath on the 7th day[17], Passover[18], and other holy days as commanded by Yahuah. The bottom line is, Yahusha did not die for a whole new religion to be implemented. When we disregard the Torah, that is exactly what we are doing.

Discarding Torah isolates Yahusha from the Father. In doing so, a false image is created. This image has a different name, ethnicity, and tells us that since He died for us, we get to pick and choose which of the Father's commandments we still need to follow. This image has also instituted a love doctrine that says if *we love everyone* and everything, even if it is an abomination before the Father, then we will be accepted.

As I was writing this, the Holy Spirit led me to Romans 1:22-23 in reference to this image, ***"Although they claimed to be wise, they became fools and exchanged the glory of the immortal God for images made to look like a mortal human being and birds, and animals and reptiles."*** Who does Scripture tell us changes his mind, leans unto their own understanding, and has a way that seems right but leads to death? Man. This "Jesus" that has been separated from both the Father and Torah is but a mere man. An *olive skinned*

---

[16] Deuteronomy 21:23, Galatians 3:13

[17] Luke 4:16

[18] Luke 22:7

individual from the *Middle East,* with a Greek name, who says he came to fulfill Yah's commandments while allowing us to disregard them. He is an invention, a fictitious character, an image. The Messiah of the Scripture tell us: ***"Do not think that I came to bring peace on earth. I did not come to bring peace but a sword. For I have come to set a man against his father, a daughter against her mother, and a daughter-in-law against her mother-in-law; and a man's enemies will be those of his own household."*** —Matthew 10:34-36

I'm always encouraging Believers to read the entire Bible including what is referred to as the Old Testament. It teaches us the character of the Father and once we realize how intentional He is, *about everything,* we will be far less likely to shrug off these un-Biblical modifications to the faith. Yahuah does not speak vain words. When He institutes something, He does so with great specificity with the expectation that it be observed accordingly. Even Yahusha, the one whom those of faith are supposed to be emulating, followed the ways of the Father, the Torah. With that said, who is man to disregard the example of the Messiah and make up their own traditions?

As Believers, we must consider the source of our interpretations and be honest about how we received the doctrine that has been passed down. More importantly, we have to remember who passed it down. Recall that so-called African Americans were initially given *slave* Bibles with missing sections. Therefore, as many of us enter these institutions of higher learning to pursue degrees in theology, divinity, and Biblical studies, we must understand that many of these doctrines are from non-Hebraic nations with zero authority to distribute a message that deviates from Scripture. We see this prophesied in Jeremiah 16:19 as it reads, ***"O Yahuah, my strength,*** *and my fortress, and my refuge in the day of affliction, the other nations shall come unto you from the ends of the earth and shall say: Surely our fathers have inherited lies, vanity, and things wherein there is no profit."* This is part of a latter-day prophecy which refers to the regathering of Yah's people as the time of the Gentiles comes to an end. It is at this point where centuries of lies will be exposed allowing the truth to prevail.

I am going to stop here on this topic. Yet, I would encourage every Believer to seek out these truths for yourself. The Scripture tells us to renew our minds and operating in spirit and truth is a part of that. Yahuah says that for a time, He winked at our ignorance, but that time is coming to an end. [19] He is calling true Believers out of Babylon. While Scripture tells us that there will be a physical manifestation of this, the preparation process starts within our hearts and minds. [20]

It is time to seek truth like never before. It is time to take a fresh look at Scripture, casting away the interpretation that we have been taught by our oppressors. The Way is simple. Religion is complex, burdensome, and wrought with contradictions as man uses it to enforce his own will. Modern church leaders would say that sin is the biggest threat to the liberty we have in Messiah, but I would argue that religion is a major contender. True Believers are born from above and with the ongoing renewal process, sin becomes less appealing until they are eventually all but dead to it. Religion has the tendency to box in the minds of even the most devout Believers and puts limitations on Elohiym. It quenches the liberty we've been granted in Messiah but many of us are unaware that we are still in bondage.

---

[19] Acts 17:30

[20] Isaiah 11:11, 2 Corinthians 6:17

As I encourage Believers to shed the excess weight of religion to embrace a genuine relationship with the Father, Son, and Holy Spirit, I want to be clear on something. I am not proposing that we look, talk, and become carbon copies of the first century Believers. We are thousands of years and cultures removed from those times. I am suggesting that we return to the ways of the Father which are timeless. This is why Yahusha was able to come hundreds of millennia after the Torah was initially given and still keep it perfectly. I highly doubt that He was wearing attire identical to the ancient Israelites or that he even spoke the exact same dialect. Paul's role and writing style was distinct from Isaiah's and other old-time prophetic writers. Yet, he still operated within the confines of Torah. This allowed him to be righteous and preserve the key elements of his Hebraic culture as the two cannot be separated from one another.

Ultimately, we want to strive to reflect the perfect ways of the Father in this dispensation so that the glory of Yah will be displayed for generations to come. This is a fulfillment of the call to be image bearers. To do so, we must know Him, intimately.

Practical Religion: Christianity & Church

The ancient Israelites were a part of a theocracy whereby there was no separation of church and state. The Torah was their religion, governance, and culture all in one. It has been ages since Yah's people were able to live in what I now see as a privileged position. In our time, religion has been used to provide the structure needed to establish a foundation for our faith.

The Most High is omniscient, seeing everything from beginning to end, from every angle. He can also use anyone and anything to carry out His purposes. Be it so, Yahuah has largely utilized the Christian religious system to engage those who truly have a heart for Him. These individuals are known as the "called out ones." They make up the generations of called out assemblies to whom the letters in Revelation 1-3 are written for. By now, it should be clear that not every member of every church who professes "Jesus" is part of this group. This is also not to say that Yah cannot call individuals from other religious factions, but what makes Christianity unique is its access to the true written and Living Word of Elohiym.

To begin, I believe it is important to state that I do not come from a background of church hurt. Most of my experiences were positive and I am grateful that my mother began taking me to services around five years old. I still have fond memories of Sunday school, youth group, choir, vacation Bible school, revival, Baptist conventions, visiting sister churches, and of course, eating the delicious food prepared by the ladies following my mom's monthly missions meetings. Our church was full of children and the pastor, deacons, teachers, and other elders loved on us. They were not only invested in our salvation but our overall well being. In hindsight, I can see that even the stern ones, or those who became so when the moment called for it, were acting out of genuine care and had our best interest at heart.

As an adult, I've visited numerous churches over the years, becoming an actual member of a handful with varying demographics. The churches I grew up in and attended post-college were Black churches through and through. Upon moving to Los Angeles, I first joined a multicultural church where the majority of the congregation was Caucasian, before attending a multicultural church with a predominantly Black membership. At my last church, however, I was one of only five Black members in the entire congregation.

As for size, the church I grew up in the '80s had around 1,500 members. This falls shy of what would be considered a "mega" church by today's standards but it was still fairly large given the time. The remainder of the churches were smaller, some with about 700 members, with others as intimate as 75.

I have worshiped with all types of people, in different regions, been involved in leadership, and served in several ministries and para ministries. I'm providing this context to emphasize my familiarity with church and religion. Being that I was called out of both by the Most High, not due to negative circumstances, positions me to offer unbiased insight. With that in mind, I want to explore the ways in which Christianity, when practiced through the lens of church culture and religion, has historically served a purpose but has also become an obstacle for Believers today.

The Benefits of Church

One of the most useful purposes that the protestant church has served in modern times is the introduction of spiritual disciplines to the individual Believer. These include worship, prayer, Bible study, and fasting. Sound churches convey the importance of these disciplines for spiritual development and provide instruction on how to put them into practice. These are invaluable because they are also the building blocks to an actual relationship with the Most High which we will discuss in further detail later.

Service to others is another value rightfully emphasized by the church. Yahusha said He came to serve, not *to be* served which is a revolutionary mindset that remains counterculture to this day.[21] After all, this is the Creator, in the flesh, saying that He came to make an offering to man. He left the glory of Heaven to offer us His gifts, knowledge, body and ultimately, His life. I will speak more on the idea of service in the next section but for now, I want to credit the church for watering this seed that Yahusha, our example, planted and fulfilled perfectly. The church can also be a discovery zone to gain understanding of our unique spiritual gifts under the guidance of experienced Believers.

Additionally, church fostered a sense of community. Although a perfect one has never existed, there were still far worse places that we all could have been 2-4 days out of the week. Houses of worship provided a consistent opportunity for Believers to turn their attention upward and inward. In many churches, regular testimonies filled the sanctuary providing a space for brothers and sisters to encourage one another as they bore witness to the goodness of Elohiym. In fact, "God is good" was a common phrase that still

---

[21] Matthew 20:28

functions as a Biblical affirmation. I can appreciate that aspect of indoctrination, as culturally, it became a part of our helmet of salvation to guard against doubt amidst trying times.

In the Baptist tradition, it was imperative to know the Word. So, by the time I was an adult I had read the entire Bible at least once or twice. Although I no longer align with much of the doctrine obtained through that denomination's interpretation, having the Living Word in me proved to be priceless. It afforded me a basic framework of understanding even if the concepts did not grow roots until much later.

Spiritual disciplines, learning the Word of Yah, identifying our unique gifting, service to others, and the character building that results from operating within community are all fundamental aspects of the faith that we continue to cultivate throughout our walk. Unfortunately, when practiced within the context of church, they often become the end goal instead of starting points. Many Believers never evolve past these basic tenets and unknowingly settle for religion with a side of relationship rather than relationship with the bit of religious structure needed to keep order. In essence, the church then becomes a hindrance instead of a springboard that should catapult us into the deeper elements of Yah.

Church as a Hindrance

Christianity's tendency to cling to the traditions of men has become a major stumbling block in the Believer's walk. Pagan holidays aside, there are countless commonplace activities and events associated with church that have absolutely nothing to do with the Most High and everything to do with man-made agendas. These recurring programs have the tendency to consume the participant's most precious resources: time, energy, and money. It also leaves room for confusion between faithful givers who are pre-occupied with church stuff and those who are, indeed, spiritual.

Religion has a subtle way of keeping us busy instead of building. We can see the manifestation of this both in the spiritual and the natural. Do we spend more time listening to sermons and attending events than we do nourishing a relationship with the Holy Spirit who promised to lead us into all understanding? How many times do shepherds have to sternly encourage their flock to read the Word for themselves? They can look out into the pews and see that despite all the sermons, programs, and events, the sheep are still in an infantile state. Furthermore, if Believers invested the same amount of time, money, and effort put into the church, directly into our communities, how much more effective change would we see?

Not only are the traditions of men deeply embedded in the church, but there is also a centering of man that occurs at both the leadership and parishioner level. Although it is not always the intent of the leader, humans tend to be idolatrous by nature. Many church goers are more excited to see the so-called "man or woman of God" than they are to hear from Yah Himself, often confusing the two. Entire programs are constructed to praise the gifts of men, given by Elohiym, with the vessel being valued above the message or even the One from whom it was sent. We see this when leaders teach messages inconsistent with the Scripture without rebuke even though we all have the same Bible and can see the error. Other times, a blind eye is turned to ministers who commit flagrant sin under the guise that he is *just a man* or the 'nobody is perfect' ideology. Meanwhile, the Scripture teaches that Believers are to be perfect as is our Father in Heaven.[22] We also know that teachers of

---

[22] Matthew 5:48

the Word are held to a higher standard, which is why they should be far and few between.[23] Yet today we find them in abundance.

In this generation, church attendees typically receive weekly sermons that are self-seeking rather than Elohiym centered. Destiny, identity, purpose, your 'best self', and other messages of the self-help variety are all prioritized over intimately knowing Yahuah. I can personally attest to the fact that despite being inundated with these messages for years, I did not receive a breakthrough in any of those areas until after I was called out of the church.

This takes me back decades ago, to when I was searching for who I was and why Yah had placed me on this earth. Around that time, Rick Warren's **Purpose Driven Life** was heavily trending in Christian circuits. Seeking clarity, I read it with great enthusiasm. However, upon completion, I couldn't quite put my finger on why I felt disappointed. While it offered some insight into gifts and serving in the local church, there was a part of me that secretly felt guilty for thinking, "Is this it?"

This leads us back to my previous point about service. There is emphasis in the Christian tradition on serving but much of it entails serving the church as an institution rather than its people. This is anti-christ or to put it mildly, the opposite of Yahusha's ministry. Of course, any establishment is going to need the help of its members to keep things running. We see this with the temple servants in the ancient days and can assume that someone had to handle the upkeep of the temples that Yahusha taught at during Sabbath. Yet, when something becomes so large and ostentatious (i.e., mega churches) it places Believers in the position of having to serve the church through countless ministries designed to keep the operation

---

[23] James 3:1

going. This 'busy work' often comes at the cost of truly deepening our relationship with our Elohiym.

Church doctrine itself is another hindrance as it is often responsible for creating 'formulas' with the most glaring one being how an individual obtains eternal salvation. Many of us were taught that if we simply believed in Jesus and recited the sinner's prayer (to cover the 'confess with your mouth' part) then our souls would be saved. It was implied that it doesn't matter what we do going forward as long as we ask forgiveness. Nor was it explained what it truly meant to know Messiah. In reality, the Scriptures give a whole list of 'Believers' who will not see the Kingdom of Heaven and we already know what Yahusha said about those whom He never knew. [24]

Other formulas include much of the prosperity messages that teach if you give *this much* then God must bless you with x,y,z. There are even blueprints for righteousness insinuating if we do everything *right* then surely, God will give us the desires of our heart. After all, that is what the Scripture says, correct? Yet, these formulas negate the developmental process designed to prepare us for what we're asking for. This mindset also inches dangerously close to idolatry as our main priority should always be maintaining a close relationship with the Father allowing thankfulness, contentment, and patience to do its perfect work.

Unfortunately, when these equations do not produce our desired outcome, disappointment, confusion, and doubt are waiting to consume the mustard seed of faith that we were clinging to. Of course, the enemy, who has been watching us play ourselves the whole time, is ready to capitalize on that.

---

[24] 1 Corinthians 6:10, Galatians 5:21, Matthew 7:21-23

The final obstacle that I want to address is that of the erroneous interpretation of Scripture. Christianity went from the Catholic leaders discouraging Believers from reading the Word for themselves to Protestants creating doctrines that a straightforward reading does not support. Even worse is when certain Scriptures are flat out ignored to create a more comfortable way of living or one that is better aligned with popular culture. I often say to my mishpacha that the Word is simple but layered. A layman taught plainly can obtain enough understanding to receive salvation and walk uprightly. Yet even a learned person must engage the Holy Spirit in order to grasp the weightier matters of the Word of Elohiym.

When Scripture is taught incorrectly, it can pacify fear instead of cultivating courage. It can breed a dangerous complacency instead of pushing one towards true obedience. Along with the misinterpretation of Scripture is the culture surrounding it. It is the unspoken ostracism that comes when one takes the Scriptures at face value instead of doing mental gymnastics to create a more palatable narrative. The fear of rejection by the mainstream, or even the truth itself, can give way to dogmatic mindsets that become extremely limiting.

Final Thoughts on Church & Religion

To be clear, I am not suggesting that people leave their church homes. What I'm offering in this writing is knowledge, perspective, or simply illumination of what you may already be starting to sense subconsciously. However, revelation by the Holy Spirit is necessary for any of this information to be effective. It's the difference from having head knowledge of the Messiah and *knowing* the Messiah which is what produces tangible change in our lives.

When it comes to how we choose to express our faith in the context of community we need to consult with the Most High directly. I am also not implying that people who attend church and practice religion cannot have a genuine relationship with Him. I know from firsthand experience that this is not true. Nevertheless, for most, it is a hindrance that is difficult to see from the inside, particularly if that is all you've ever known.

What I am saying is that the Christian religion expressed through "the church" has a flawed foundation, perpetuates false doctrine, stunts the spiritual growth of Believers, and holiness does not exist in this institution at large. When I say holy, I am referring to when something is **set apart** for a divine and sacred purpose. The house of Elohiym is to be a place to worship our Creator. A place where we learn about Him and how to please Him. This also includes how we treat one another. It is not a marketplace, an entertainment center, or a place for man to be glorified. Nor should it primarily focus on how to thrive according to worldly standards or be used as a catch all to solve all of man's problems.

Perhaps it's my naivety, but I do believe that some of these ministers mean well. Yet all of us have been infected with the disease of religion, which can put leaders in the position of unwittingly treating the symptom rather than the actual illness. The illness being this narcissistic tendency to focus on the desires of self rather than what Elohiym requires of us. Although obedience is our reasonable service, it also places us on the receiving end of all the good things that Yah desires to lavish upon us. Psalm 84:11 reminds us that He withholds no good thing from those who walk uprightly. And as 1 Corinthians 2:9 declares, ***"Eye has not seen, nor ear heard, neither have entered into the heart of man, the things which Elohiym has prepared for those that love Him."***

It all comes full circle; loving Him is proven through obedience, and obedience flows from knowing Him through His Word. Without this foundation, the traditions of men await us as a snare, luring us into a false righteousness with a false Elohiym.

To be clear, the Scripture speaks of giving honor to whom it is due. There is also nothing wrong with equipping Believers to develop holistically. However, it should not be mixed with our worship and the Father should always be the priority. When our allegiance is wholly transferred to Yahuah and the coming Kingdom of Yahusha, the strongholds of religion or church will naturally loosen. From that place, we can worship Him in spirit and truth and count on Him, in time, to lead us into a community that is suitable for the season that we're in. I believe that the Most High has people everywhere and many are on assignment. It is up to us to ensure that we are connected to Him in such a way that we are where we are supposed to be at the right time.

My goal in the following chapters is to help place Believers on a path that will ultimately leave them Spirit filled and whole. Above all else, the aim is to identify and remove hindrances and put into practice that which allows us to truly know our Elohiym and remain in constant communication with Him. This positions us to be not only Spirit filled but Spirit led.

We began at the macro level with Christianity and the church because it's important to know that the enemy is extremely strategic using tradition, familiarity, and things that seem right to distract us from The Way. Matthew 7:13-14 says ***"Enter through the narrow gate. For wide is the gate and broad is the road that leads to destruction, and many enter. But small is the gate and narrow the road that leads to life, and only a few find it."*** The church, through the religious system of Christianity, has largely become the broad road. However, that does not nullify the Creator's call for His people to remain set apart and holy. Therefore if the church is no longer on the narrow path then one must seek Yah for direction. To do so, we must move beyond religion and create intimacy with the Most High. With that said, the reminder of this book will be dedicated to the faith walk of the individual seeking to achieve this.

CHAPTER 4

Intimacy with the Most High

From the very beginning it has been the desire of the Most High to have a close intimate relationship with those made in His image. He walked in the cool of the day with Adam and Eve in the garden and later with faithful servants such as Enoch and Abraham.[25] Enoch was so close to Him that he never saw death and was instead taken up into the presence of Elohiym. Abraham's friendship with El Shaddai resulted in the birth of a chosen nation through his lineage with a covenant that is still intact until this day.[26] The Most High also wants intimacy with His people as a whole. We see this centuries later when He wished to speak to the Israelites directly on Mount Sinai. Yet they shrunk back in fear and sent Moses to go on their behalf.[27] Yahuah even intended to be their King, but in their desire to be like the other nations, they requested an earthly ruler.[28]

I can only imagine how frustrating it is to create something for relationship, breathe life into it, only to then be rejected by that said thing. A part of having intimacy with the Most High is understanding that He is an emotional being with feelings. At the time of this writing, we are studying the book of Jeremiah. The amount of hurt, anger, grief, and longing expressed by Yahuah is perplexing, amazing, and heartbreaking all at the same time.

---

[25] Genesis 3:8

[26] Genesis 17:1-19

[27] Exodus 20:18-21

[28] 1 Samuel 8:5

Perplexing because who are we that He is mindful of us? Amazing because He is. Heartbreaking because, in most cases, His passion for us is not reciprocated. Over time, the enemy has done an excellent job of using sin, doubt, fear, and discontentment to drive a wedge between Yah and His people. And still, the evidence of His longing to be intimately acquainted with us remains. The birth, death, and resurrection of His beloved Son being the ultimate manifestation of His desire for reconciliation.[29]

Intimacy is defined as having a sense of familiarity of a personal or private nature. Nothing has the potential to be more intimate than our relationship with the Most High. Relationships with our spouses, parents, and children all pale in comparison. No one knows us better than our Maker, including ourselves. He had a vision of us before we were born and I believe this is the lens through which He views us. He works tirelessly on our behalf to get us to live up to the vision of perfection that He imagined before we were in our mother's womb.[30] I imagine Him patiently observing us fighting our flesh in the midst of a dark world as we make our way back to Him. He is aware of our future, past, strengths, limitations, and all our secrets. He knows our words before they are spoken and understands the context of our thoughts.[31]

For some, this may seem intrusive, but I find it liberating. I am finally able to be 100% authentic because to not be real with someone with divine x-ray vision is nonsensical. He not only thoroughly understands me, but He is wholeheartedly invested in my well-being. He is all knowing, enabling Him to be the ultimate Counselor. He owns the entire universe so everything that I need is

---

[29] 2 Corinthians 5:19-20
[30] Jeremiah 1:5
[31] Psalm 139

at His fingertips. All He requires is love expressed through obedience and for us to simply ask with His will in mind.

However, this intimacy is reserved for a certain group of people. The Scripture says that Yah makes it rain on the just and unjust, which refers to the general grace given to all human beings. [32] Yet, John 9:31 tells us that the Father does not hear the prayers of sinners. Therefore, if we are not His, then we are subjecting our lives solely to time and chance that happens to all men. [33] Intimacy with the Most High is for those who have agreed to surrender their lives to Him. Surrendering our lives means to turn away from the things that He hates and to pursue what He says is good. It's seeking Him out for guidance as we go about our daily lives. It's dying to our lower self in exchange for the supreme version of ourselves that He envisions.

The prerequisite to surrender is trust. We must remember that the enemy has used fear and doubt to sow seeds of distrust in us towards our Elohiym since the days of Eden. [34] In today's world, we doubt that if we surrender to Him, our lives will be as fulfilling as the ambitions we have in mind for ourselves. We fear that if we let the Most High select our spouse that they will be ugly, dull, or it will take too long. Most importantly we doubt that He really is enough. We fear that if we fully commit to Him that we will miss out on something. But with Yah as my witness, I can assure you that these are all lies from the pits of hell. They are the types of lies that take form when you know *of* someone but do not know them intimately.

---

[32] Matthew 5:45

[33] Ecclesiastes 9:11

[34] Genesis 3:1-13

We may even judge Yah based on the lives of people who claim to know Him without understanding that there are levels to this. We must bear in mind that we are all unique individuals and someone else may be content with a life that would leave us wanting. He is a dynamic Elohiym, and as beings created in His image, so are we. There are no two humans that are the same on this earth. Similar, but never completely identical. Because He is an intentional Father, He deals with us according to our individual characteristics in tandem with His ultimate plan for our lives. Any decent mother or father figure will tell you that you cannot parent multiple children in the exact same way. Of course, there are guidelines that exist across the board but personalities, temperament, abilities, short-comings and even predispositions are all factored into how a parent interacts with each child. How much more so will it be with our Heavenly Father from Whose eyes nothing is hidden?[35]

This relationship is not for everyone. In one of His parables, Yahusha talks about how many are called but few are chosen.[36] The chosen hear the call of the Shepherd and answer it accordingly.[37] In fact, the *answering* becomes their ultimate life mission. The journey doesn't begin at birth, but at the moment we surrender to The Way the Father has made for us to be restored to Him. That is through the Messiah, Yahusha Ha'Mashiach, whom much of the world refers to as Jesus Christ.[38] He is Elohiym in the flesh, the only one who was qualified to pay the price for man's sin. The Word is clear that no one comes to the Father but through the Son.[39]

---

[35] Hebrews 4:13
[36] Matthew 22:1-14
[37] John 10:26-27
[38] John 3:16
[39] John 14:6

It is by accepting the sacrifice of the Messiah and making a conscious choice to turn away from the things forbidden in Scripture that we are now fit to receive the Holy Spirit.[40] The Spirit empowers us to live according to Scripture as the set-apart people of Yahuah.[41] This is the beginning of true intimacy with the Most High. Through His Son, we are now able to approach His throne boldly as sons and daughters of the King.[42] We can refer to Him as Abba[43] and our souls enter a supernatural peace knowing that in both life and death we are secure in His hands.

As our spirit man develops, we are far less anxious, opting to express gratitude for what we have. We are able to make our petitions in faith knowing that our Heavenly Father hears us and will answer according to His will. As we mature, we realize that life will not be perfect, recalling that the Messiah said we will have tribulation in this world.[44] We accept that our faith will be tested. After all, it's easy to be devoted when all is well. We know that some of these tests come from the Father and others He allows for His own purposes. Either way, every situation makes way for our Elohiym to show up for us and, in turn, our bond is strengthened. We understand that His glory is used to draw men unto Him, and we are willing to offer up ourselves as living sacrifices to this end. Finally, we humble ourselves to the fact that we may not fully understand why certain things happen. Still, we remain steadfast, patiently awaiting what time unveils, even as we make peace with the mysteries that may never be answered in this lifetime.

---

[40] Acts 2:38

[41] 1 Thessalonians 4:7-8

[42] Hebrews 4:16

[43] Galatians 4:6

[44] John 16:33

This is a spiritual overview of the life of a Believer. However, there is a lot that happens in the midst of these things, and it is Yah's desire that we go deeper in Him beyond simply overcoming. His Elect are to go from glory to glory.[45] That includes evolving from a strictly parental relationship where we are simply getting our earthly needs met. Our Elohiym is the most dynamic, creative, multi-dimensional infinite Being that has ever existed. He desires to reveal parts of Himself to us as well as secret things with those that He can trust.[46] He seeks to expand our minds and abilities in ways that we did not think possible as we are being transformed to perfection.

While the Bible is foundational, Yahuah never intended for us to merely read about Him, marveling at the prophets of old or those who walked with Messiah in the first century. He desires to move powerfully in our lives today, performing great exploits through us just the same. In fact, Yahusha says that we will do even greater things than what He has done.[47] Be it so, I would argue that the greatest level of settling occurs within our spiritual lives. Every aspect of our existence should be entwined with our spirituality as we live out our faith instead of merely hearing, being spectators, and taking part in programs. We severely limit ourselves when we sequester our spiritual lives to religious services and praying for our basic needs to be met. We will not go beyond the status quo by completing daily devotionals and attending weekly meetings. In many places in the Word, Yahuah tells us to seek Him diligently and inquire of Him. This takes time, patience, effort, and practiced discernment.

---

[45] 2 Corinthians 3:18
[46] Jermiah 33:3
[47] John 14:12

In all His glory, the Father has many sides to Him including a sense of humor. Trust me, there are no inside jokes better than with someone who knows you intimately, inside out. Religious constructs can restrict us from experiencing Him outside of rigid ideals.

One common misconception is that this is a one-sided deal where it is all about the Creator. While this is true, our very essence is found within Him. He has intentionally designed our purpose, destiny, and the highest version of ourselves to be hidden in Him. There are no short-cuts. It is an ironic arrangement in that the more we get to know Him, the more we get to know ourselves and the mysteries of His plan for our lives become unlocked. When we try to circumvent our Heavenly Father to get to these things, we will come up short every time. Regardless of how much success we've had in our personal lives or even in ministry, if our foundation is not in Him, then we are operating in a lesser version of ourselves at best, and in a complete counterfeit form at worst.

We must remember that the gifts are without repentance so if Yah placed a powerful voice-box inside of you, you may very well be able to amass wealth and fame. The question becomes, what will that profit you if your soul is lost in the process? You may be a gifted charismatic speaker, and in some cases, that alone can fill up a church, but are you in His will? We often measure our success by worldly or *Christian* standards instead of knowing the heart of the Father and what pleases Him.

Cultivating intimacy with the Most High will also initiate fresh experiences with Him. In this season I am experiencing Him as a watchful Shepherd. This is a busy season for me where sometimes I have concerns that linger in the back of my mind, subconsciously. Yahuah, in His graciousness, has been providing answers to these unspoken prayers. This happens simultaneously so that the answer and the need are revealed at the same time, leaving me awestruck that the matter was resolved before I was fully aware that it existed.

Recently, I found myself quietly sulking over a promise I felt Yahuah was taking too long to fulfill. I say 'quietly' because I had not shared it with anyone, or even mentioned it in prayer. In fact, I didn't fully realize that I had grown salty (not in a good way) until Yah lovingly confronted me about it. I knew that I had been short with Him and lacking my usual zeal for our private time, but I had not connected the dots as to why. Sure, I was doing my typical acknowledgements and general prayers, but I had not been setting aside time to really sit and commune with Him. However, He sent me a word through another Believer via YouTube that addressed my issue verbatim and gave me the perspective I needed to get back on track. It was at that moment that I realized that I had grown weary in waiting and it was affecting our relationship. However, the Watchful Shepherd knew. He was observing me the whole time. Instead of getting annoyed with my impatience He sent a restorative word.

Another example dealt with a loved one who needed financial assistance. Yah had already been putting it on my heart to bless this person, but it kept slipping my mind. Not to mention, they also lived in a different state. Sure enough, within a week or so, He rearranged my work schedule in such a way that I crossed paths with this person, and our conversation served as a clear reminder of what I was originally supposed to do.

This is the kind of intimacy I'm referring to, where He sees beyond the surface and knows my heart's desire isn't to neglect prayer, cling to offense, or resist releasing what He's asked of me. He knows that I have a lot on my mind and that I am a woman with emotions that overcome me at times. He knows I deal with the distractions of the modern world just like anyone else. But because He is intentionally watching what is going on with me, He makes provisions even when I'm not fully aware of my own needs. He is a present help, ordering my steps and ensuring that I stay on the path that He has placed me on. He is not angrily waiting to punish me for being a mere mortal. Psalms 103:13-14 gently reminds us *"Like as a father pities his children, so Yahuah pities them that fear Him. For He knows our frame; He remembers that we are dust."* Nothing compares to the watchful care and compassion of the Most High cultivated through an intimate relationship with Him.

PART II

Hindrances to Intimacy
with the Most High

CHAPTER 5

The Religious Spirit

We have spoken at length about religion from a systematic perspective, but the religious spirit will be explored in the context of the individual. It entails one who presents outwardly as a Believer, but lacks true love, passion, and desire for the Most High.[48] It is what this generation would refer to as "performative religion." I began with this hindrance because it is one that is rampant yet easily missed within faith-based communities. These are those who acknowledge Christ as their savior, attend religious gatherings, serve in some form of ministry, give, pray, and read the Bible. Because they check all the necessary boxes, they believe that they are saved from hell, and their spiritual lives are solid. For the sake of humility, they will say that they are not perfect but would find themselves hard pressed should you ask how Yah is moving in their lives or what recent revelation they have received from the Holy Spirit.

Although prayer and reading the Bible are key to having a relationship with the Most High, it is possible to do so in vain. Our prayers can be selfish, superficial, and out of sync with the will of the Father. We can read simply for the sake of reading or even do so without understanding. We may even read from an informative perspective rather than an authoritative one. This will not compel us to put what we've read into practice, particularly when it is something outside of our comfort zone. When spiritual disciplines remain on the surface level, they become ritualistic in nature

---

[48] Matthew 22:37

(religious) and our relationship with Yah becomes stale and, in some instances, non-existent. Religion becomes our god, and this god justifies our wrong doings, is satisfied with our shallow worship, and never requires more of us than we are willing to give.

A religious spirit will reveal itself through interactions with Believers and non-believers alike. With non-believers, it may come in the form of how we witness. Are we truly sharing about the Father and the Son or is the main emphasis on getting people to join our church/assembly? There is nothing wrong with inviting someone to a gathering, but that need not always be the starting point nor the end goal. Yahusha's command was to *go and make disciples* not recruit people to come to the temple.

A judgemental attitude towards non-believers is also a sign of a religious spirit. Scripture clearly instructs us not to take this approach as non-believers are worldly, void of the Holy Spirit and their actions will reflect as such.[49] When we hold them to the same measure of accountability as a Believer, we are expecting them to walk in Biblical righteousness according to their own strength, which is impossible. Surely, one can be a "good person" according to the world's standards, but without the Helper we are not equipped to strive towards the perfection that Messiah commanded.[50]

This is not to say we turn a blind eye to wickedness, nor do we condone it. However, if we are casting judgment without pointing non-believers to The One who can free them from the strongholds of sin, then we must be honest in evaluating our motives. Are we truly intending for our words and actions to lead them to Elohiym or is it to make ourselves feel superior?

---

[49] 1 Corinthians 5:12
[50] John 14:16-17

Amongst Believers, a religious spirit can show up in being overly critical towards one another especially regarding topics that the Bible does not specifically address. Or, as with the Pharisees, it holds other Believers to a standard higher than what is prescribed in Scripture. Yes, the Word should inform all our choices, but we must allow people to work out their own salvation within the gray areas. We are to be mindful of becoming obstacles to those with weak consciences, but we also should not lord our personal convictions over one another.[51] Religious spirits are often unbalanced in this area.

An individual with a religious spirit will place the culture of Christianity, their denomination, or even what their church considers acceptable above the actual commandments of Yah.[52] Certain traditions, holidays, and lifestyle choices would fall into this category. We also see this when it comes to political affiliations. Someone with a religious spirit will vehemently proclaim that a particular party is aligned with "Christian values" and there may be some general truth to that. However, all political parties fall miserably short of Biblical standards. Therein lies the issue; confusion between what is Christian and what is Biblical. A religious spirit will have a difficult time telling the difference.

Finally, hypocrisy and a religious spirit go hand in hand. Surely, we all have weaknesses and areas that need refinement, but I am referring to something more pervasive in nature. This is an individual that has not merely stumbled, but is walking in consistent rebellion to what they profess to believe in. Claiming to know Messiah and fulfilling the outward appearances of a Believer, while

---

[51] Romans 14
[52] Mark 7:8-9

living contrary to the Word, is another example of a performative religion.

A religious spirit is dangerous because it is rooted in self-deception and hidden by pride. Operating off the "checked boxes" paradigm, we can deceive ourselves into thinking we are spiritually sound. This leaves little room for growth and presents a false narrative to new Believers. It suggests that the pinnacle of our faith is memorizing Scripture and being an active part of a ministry. If we behave as if, because we've read 66 books of the Bible, we now understand everything about our Elohiym then there is no progress left to be made.

Someone with a religious spirit will not readily admit this. In fact, there is a good chance they will not be consciously aware of it because they are surrounded by those with similar mindsets. As leaders recycle the same sermons year after year, one with a religious spirit will not seek out anything beyond that. Their pride deceives them into thinking that their current understanding is conclusive. Often when unfamiliar information is presented, even that which can be supported by Scripture, it is immediately shut down and will not even be brought before the Father as a question.

It is important to understand the role that fear plays when it comes to religious spirits. Since these individuals' faith is based on a formula that they believe secures salvation, they feel threatened by anything that does not fit the equation. Unfortunately, this cognitive dissonance fused with pride, fear, and lack of faith creates a spiritual elixir that will prevent someone from trusting in the Holy Spirit enough to seek out truth; thus, rendering them stagnant.

The worst part of having a religious spirit is its ability to stifle our relationship with the Father and how it attempts to do the same for others. Not only does it thrive from religious checklists, personal and cultural opinions, fear, pride, and legalism but it also restricts the Creator in how He can interact with us. A person who limits spiritual encounters to the "Biblical times" may not be open to the way that Yah wants to connect with us in this present dispensation. I've noticed that it is typically those who have never had a prophetic dream, vision, or spoken in tongues that attempt to discredit these channels of communication. Instead of asserting what is so for the entire body of Messiah, they should simply acknowledge that they have not personally experienced these gifts.

Yahuah doesn't change and we can learn about His ways through His Word. However, He Himself warns us that our understanding will be limited.[53] We must also acknowledge that while the Word is our foundation, and while Yah will never contradict His Word, He is not limited to only what we see in Scripture. The Word was given to us so that we would learn His nature but it is preposterous to behave as if we will know exactly how He moves in this age when there are things that simply did not exist during Biblical times. There is only one exception to there being *"Nothing new under the sun"* and that is us. We are new, a tiny blip in the grand scheme of time. Everything we learn about in history, our present time, and the days to come is news to us. This is why we must seek Him and be open to how He may choose to connect with us through the various channels of this age.

Ultimately, a religious spirit hinders our intimacy with the Most High. It causes us to be focused on the wrong things: outward appearances of piousness rather than inner holiness; preoccupation with what non-believers are doing, being hyper critical of fellow

---

[53] Isaiah 55:8-9

Believers, and holding on to preconceived notions of our Creator instead of getting to know Him for ourselves.

CHAPTER 6
Pride

An entire book can be written on pride and the effects it has on both the spiritual and material aspects of our lives. Although we will discuss several other barriers to our relationship with the Most High, if we look closely enough, we can see that pride is the driving force behind many, if not all of them. In the last chapter we considered how a religious spirit may cause one to assume that they are thriving spiritually because they have checked several religious boxes. Pride is at the center of this belief, bringing us to the first point: **Pride creates blind spots where we are unable to see ourselves.** According to Scripture, this opens the door to deception as it reads, ***"Let no one fool himself. If someone among you thinks he is wise (by this world's standards), let him become "foolish," so that he may become really wise."*** —1 Corinthians 3:18

Pride puts a wedge between us and the Most High. As with any parent, He desires to lead and guide us. If we operate as if we already know everything, it makes us unteachable. The word *operate* is intentionally used because any sane person will admit that they don't know everything. It is our actions that expose our subconscious belief that our current understanding is sufficient. This is why it is important for us to examine our behavior, including our speech, against what we believe to be true about ourselves.

When operating with an openness to learn, we must also be careful not to allow pride to cause us to *lean unto our own understanding.*[54] Our brains are designed to organize information in a way that builds upon the knowledge that we already possess. However, when it comes to the Kingdom, we often see that the Most High operates in ways different than what we would expect. In 1 Kings, Elohiym was teaching Elijah how to discern His voice. Elijah was reasonably searching for the Creator's voice in the strong wind, in an earthquake, and within the fire. Ultimately, His voice was described as "still and small".[55] Yahuah competes with no one and nothing; not even our own incessant thoughts about how we see things or even how we believe *He* sees things.

When we become too attached to current ways of thinking and believing, we may experience hurt and confusion when it does not produce the outcome that we expect. As a result, we direct our frustrations towards the Most High because, surely, we have done everything right. We secretly believe that He's mean, isn't listening, or just doesn't care. This can be prevented by avoiding a prideful attitude about our own perspectives and levels of understanding. Pride masked as ultra independence can also hinder our relationship with the Father. There is a saying that goes, "we make plans and ask God to bless it". Instead, we should ask Yah what the plan is, and request His help in bringing it to fruition. Dependance on Him requires us to subdue our innate prideful assumption that we know what's best for us.

When I initially sensed that I was being prepared for marriage, I grappled with the idea of whether or not God chooses our spouse. I've never had a problem meeting guys, however, meeting a *godly* man was a different story. There were eligible men of faith in my vicinity, but I wasn't even remotely interested in any of them. To

---

[54] Proverbs 3:5-6

[55] 1 Kings 19:11-13

further complicate matters, this particular time period bled into the early days of Covid-19 during the lockdowns. This made the advice of well-meaning people who encouraged me to attend faith-based events to meet men null and void.

Next, they steered me towards online dating. While I had never done it before, I didn't have anything against it. In fact several of my friends had gone that route, and it actually seemed fun. So, I decided to give it a shot which lasted all of 2-3 weeks. The swift ending came when one site matched me with my psycho ex-boyfriend that I had dated over a decade prior. Among other things, that was my sign from Yah that this was not His plan for me. Looking back, I can't help but be amused at this brief chapter of me trying to figure this out.

After declaring the devil a liar and deleting my profiles, I decided to put dating to the side and continue to focus on my relationship with my Elohiym. Soon after, I found myself watching a pastor online who spoke something that put an end to all of my confusion. He said when it comes to choosing our spouse, we should be seeking God's preference. That made so much sense to me. Of course, there are tons of people that I could marry and possibly have a form of happiness with, but who does Yah prefer me to be with? This singular bit of advice proved to be life changing for me. Not to mention that this principle can be applied to everything, not just marriage.

I came into agreement with this word immediately and communicated to the Most High that I wanted His preference. I'll be honest, after seeing who was available online, I had told Him that I was also okay with being single indefinitely. However, me trusting Him enough to prefer His preference led to an immense amount of breakthrough in this area of my life. The story is still in progress, but

I look forward to sharing the testimony when Yah brings it all together!

We have been given free reign to strike out on our own and make choices pertaining to our careers, spouses, where we live, etc. Our decisions may even yield satisfactory results, but do they align with our destinies and the best possible outcome for our lives? Only the Father knows that. If we are too prideful to solicit His direction, then we are selling ourselves short. We are also missing out on one of the fundamental purposes of life itself: *to fulfill His specific plan for us as individuals.* This is only achievable to the highest degree with the help of our Maker. Furthermore, the Most High is principled and faithful to the agreements He makes. One of those agreements is that of free will. He does not force us to do anything, including seek His counsel. If we behave as if we have everything together then He is just to leave us to our own devices. [56]

This isn't to say He won't respond to us when we come to the painful realization that our choices are subpar, and we need His assistance. All of us get ourselves into a mess at one time or another and depend on His grace and mercy to not hold it against us. His willingness to help should actually lessen this pattern of straying away as we realize that the solution always lies with Him and life would run a lot smoother if we would consult Him first. Constantly making bad decisions where He has to bail us out puts us in an endless cycle of being rescued from the pit only to fall back in again. In the grand scheme of things, it would appear that this is a normal part of the human experience. After all, Yah is our salvation. Nevertheless, we *should* be going from glory to glory. Not from pothole to sinkhole and back again.

---

[56] Proverbs 1:29-31

The Israelites provide an exhausting example of this throughout Scripture. While their story is still unfolding, Scripture shows us that they could never really thrive like Yah intended them to. They were given special favor by the Most High that He might be glorified through them and draw all nations to Himself. Yet, they kept going their own way, causing them to fall into all types of traps that prevented them from reaching their full potential as a nation.

The Most High knows the beginning from the end so He knew in advance that He would have to send a Messiah to eventually restore His people. However, I do not believe that it was His perfect will for them to suffer to the extent that they did due to seeking independence from Him and His ways, which is ultimately sin. This is still not His perfect will for us as individuals. He would much rather us acknowledge Him in all of our ways and be guided into the specific plan that He has for us. Following Him doesn't guarantee a life void of hardship but we need not invite unnecessary adversity by living independently from His will. As we will discuss later, depending on Him will strengthen our relationship as we begin to see Him make impossible ways for us in real time. Honestly, it's addictive.

Finally, pride can hinder our relationship with the Most High when it comes to our dealings with others. Yes, the Holy Spirit is our ultimate teacher, but there are times when He uses other people to assist in our learning process. As we mature in our relationship with Him, He will often use people to confirm what He has already spoken to us in private. Although Yah can use anyone, the vessel may not always be who we expect. We can also guarantee that the vessel will not be perfect as none of us are. If we possess a prideful attitude towards those that we perceive as younger/older, less spiritual or biblically astute, then we may be missing out on what Yah is attempting to teach us through that individual.

To be clear, we don't have to come into agreement with every message but we would be wise to always consider the source. Still, a prideful heart often disqualifies the messenger, not by the standards of the Most High, but by our own. He uses the foolish things of this world to confound the wise.[57] When pride blinds us, we risk missing Him entirely, unable to recognize that He may be speaking through a person we least expect…or even, as Scripture reminds us, through a donkey.[58] Without this intervention, we may continue in the wrong direction and then, like clockwork, blame Him when things don't go well.

This list isn't exhaustive as it's simply meant to be an aid in the self examination process that we should be doing in an effort to remain pure of heart. However, there is one major underlying reason why pride is so damaging to our relationship with the Most High: He hates it.[59] He even goes so far as to call those that are arrogant in heart an abomination.[60] On the list of 7 things given to us that He hates, a **_haughty look_** is number one.[61] This includes all of our eye rolling, serving face, and smirks when we think we know something. If He hates a prideful look, how do we think He feels about a prideful heart? There are over 150 Scriptures referencing pride and how He responds to those who walk in it. It literally repels Him. If for no other reason, our love and desire to be close to Him should be motivation to actively steer clear of pride.

---

[57] 1 Corinthians 1:27
[58] Numbers 22:21-39
[59] Proverbs 8:13
[60] Proverbs 16:5
[61] Proverbs 6:16-17

I can only imagine that a part of the reason He hates pride so much is that it reminds Him of a certain beautiful being that He created perfectly. This creature was imbedded with choice jewels of Heaven and supreme vocal cords. They allowed him to emit a praise so excellent that he was chosen to lead the choirs of Shamayim. This being became so enamored with himself that even having beheld the matchless glory of Elohiym, he determined that he was worthy to be exalted *above* the Most High. What took place after that was unforgivable and made him a permanent enemy in the eyes of Yahuah. This all began with the seed of pridefulness. We do well to avoid any semblance of this trait if we desire to be close to our Heavenly Father as it is downright devilish.

CHAPTER 7

Fear

The Most High would have it that we fear nothing and no one except Him. I have heard it said that when the word fear is used in Scripture, it is more so referring to respect and reverence. The Hebrew word for fear is yare' which means to revere but it also literally means fear and to frighten. The word occurs 331 times in Scripture and in many cases, it is used when we are being commanded to not be afraid of something.

El Shaddai is omnipresent, omniscient, and omnipotent and we would be wise to fear Him knowing that He alone holds the power to destroy our bodies and souls.[62] However, it is impossible to have a thriving intimate relationship with Yahuah when fear is our driving emotion. Many of us are fearful because we don't take Yah at His Word. We look around at the brokenness of this world and allow our limited perspective to cause us to doubt His goodness.

We compare ourselves to others and wonder when the other shoe is going to drop in our lives. *When will I be the one to suffer that great loss of a spouse or child? When will it be my turn to receive the diagnosis? When will I have to experience losing everything I've worked for my entire life leaving my family and I at rock bottom?* These do not have to be conscious thoughts but if our minds are not renewed, then we can trust that these fears are lying dormant, secretly waiting to be proven correct.

---

[62] Matthew 10:28

We are also fearful because we know where we've been. We are acutely aware of all that the Father overlooked and forgave to bring us into relationship with Him. Although we have been forgiven, a part of us believes that at some point the Most High is going to get revenge for our past iniquities. Our lack of forgiveness of ourselves leads us to believe that, if indeed this is the case, it is justifiable.

Some of us live in a state of fear regarding our eternal destiny. One of my biggest pet peeves is when Believers speak as if we can never truly know if we are in good standing with the Most High. I cringe each time I hear someone say, "I hope I make it into the Kingdom." It bothers me because it subtly insinuates that Yahuah has a secret criteria that He is using to judge us. I am one that leans towards intuition and feeling, however, there is a very logical side of me as well that occasionally takes over. This is one of those times. If, through Messiah and the power of the Holy Spirit we are intentionally keeping His commandments, which are simply detailed instructions on how to love the Most High with all our heart, soul, strength, and mind and to love our neighbors as ourselves, then why are we unsure of our destiny?

Psalm 121 offers a clear and powerful picture of how our Elohiym responds to those who seek Him. The final verses, 7 and 8, beautifully capture the heart of the chapter: ***"Yahuah shall guard you from all evil; He shall guard your soul. Yahuah shall guard your going out and your coming in, from this time forth and even forevermore."*** In short, if we are willing to be kept, demonstrated by obedience, then Yah is faithful to keep *us*. So, does this fear of damnation come from an unbalanced understanding of grace or is Yah a liar? Will He switch up on us on judgment day?

While the root of these thoughts can be traced back to insecurity and feelings of unworthiness, it is still an affront to the Most High to not take Him at His Word. It is unbelief and reflects a lack of trust that He is who He says He is. These fears are understandable, however, if not addressed, they will have an adverse effect on our relationship with our Heavenly Father. Instead, we may begin to have a relationship with the Bible or the *laws, statutes, and commandments* rather than the Creator of them. Fear will hinder the intimacy that our soul longs for with Him whether we are aware of it or not.

How Fear Hinders

As mentioned earlier, fear is rooted in unbelief, and that alone places us at a significant spiritual disadvantage. Even if we were to suffer a great loss of some sort, be it a loved one, our health, or wealth, do we not trust the Most High to see us through it? It is insulting to Him when our fear supersedes our belief. We see stunning examples of this in Psalm 78 and Psalm 106:24 when the Most High unleashed His wrath on the Israelites because they doubted His salvation and His promise, respectively.

When our fear outweighs our belief, it exposes how we truly see our Creator. Anything that is less than perfect, all powerful, and faithful is a lie. This is not to shame any of us who may occasionally have these thoughts, but we cannot not stay there. Doing so will allow the enemy to gain a foothold into our minds that seeps down into our hearts to create a paralyzing stronghold.

As mentioned previously, fear can be at the root of a religious spirit. Again, it is tied to the formula that we have put our trust in, rather than the work of Messiah. Therefore, anything that does not coincide with said formula feels like a threat to our salvation and is quickly shunned. The irony of this is that many of these irrational fears are not Biblical. They are a result of systemic religious brainwashing and or a misinterpretation of Scripture.

An example of this would be limiting ourselves to only 66 books of the Bible. Earlier versions of the written Word such as the Ethiopian Bible which is considered to be the oldest and most complete, includes 15 additional books called **The Apocrypha**. These books even remained in the King James version as late as 1885, until gentile Protestants had them removed while having no authority to do so. Some of these books are also referenced in the canon. [63]

What we fail to realize is that our Hebrew ancestors authored **many** books, several of which are under the lock and key of the Vatican. The absence of this literature leaves a void in historical context which the enemy has used to distort the truth. It is similar to when "slave Bibles" were given to the enslaved people of the U.S. during the Transatlantic Slave Trade. This revised version, which equated to most of the "Old" Testament and half of the "New" Testament, was said to have removed any passages that would inspire liberation. Thankfully, the Most High is faithful in ensuring that the parts required to lead us to salvation remained present throughout the ages. Therefore, it is important to state that reading or not reading what the enemy has kept from us at any given time is not related to salvation. However, it is related to a greater understanding of Yahuah and by extension, intimacy with Him.

As I may have opened a can of worms, I consider it to be irresponsible for me not to give the following disclaimer. I would recommend that everyone get a firm understanding of the 66 books of the Bible before exploring anything else. Furthermore, we must

---

[63] Joshua 10:13, Jude

be led by the *Ruach* in all things. The Holy Spirit knows when we are ready for more and what **meat** may be too strong for us to digest at our current level of development.

If we find ourselves leery of some newly introduced information, there is nothing wrong with asking Yah if this is something we should investigate. We can trust that He will answer, and we should be patient enough not to move forward until He does. For the record, I have read the entire Apocrypha and nothing in there shook my faith in the least bit. If anything, it strengthened it by providing a more robust understanding.

Additionally, fear affects the way we interact with others. This can, by proxy, hinder our relationship with the Most High. Avoiding controversial subjects or isolating ourselves from Believers who have different perspectives than us is an example of this. I am not referring to things that are anti-Messiah in nature or that are flagrantly against the Word of Yah. However, if we are too fearful to have a reasonable degree of open mindedness, then we may be limiting the avenues in which He may be trying to minister to us or bring us to a deeper level of understanding. All of this can lead to us having a very rigid view of our Elohiym.

Above all, fear will impact our communication with the Most High. As I have mentioned before, sometimes we can hear Yah in our own tone. This is why, at times, it can be challenging to distinguish our own voice from His. Yet some Believers, paralyzed by the fear of getting it wrong, choose not to listen for the voice of Yah at all. Unfortunately, this mindset is often reinforced by ministers who teach that the Most High speaks *only* through His written Word. It is an unbiblical fear-based tactic meant to ensure that people do not venture outside the boundaries of what said leader deems acceptable. In plain language, it is a control mechanism. I would also argue that in some cases, the minister means well and may view this as a means of protection.

However, Psalms 24 tells us, ***"To Yahuah is the earth, and the fulness thereof; the world, and they that dwell therein."*** Therefore, He can use anything and anyone at any given time to communicate to us, and He does. This includes, but is not limited to, His written Word. Unfortunately, this fear-based belief causes some Believers to have a relationship with Yah that solely consists of worship and praying for the needs of themselves and others.

Many of us are afraid to question the Most High. While I'm not necessarily referring to questioning His judgment, we do have examples of that in Scripture. Right out the gate in Genesis, we see Abraham blatantly asking if He, the Judge of all the world, will do what is right?[64] In the book of Job, we see him questioning El Shaddai as to why so much evil has befallen upon him and his family? Job got checked, but the Most High harkened to Abraham. Yet, neither of them was punished, cut off or sent to hell for having an honest dialogue with their Creator. Nevertheless, it is imperative that we exercise reverence as both men did when addressing the Most High. Yes, He is a friend to us but He's not ***one of our little friends.***

Honesty is paramount because what relationship can be built when we are not being real with our concerns and how we feel? Still, some Believers are afraid to ask Yahuah, the Creator of the Universe, a mere question even from a place of genuine curiosity. This is the type of mindset that ensues when you have a relationship with a religion and not the One True Living Elohiym. It is also evidence that either we don't read the Word, or we don't genuinely

---

[64] Genesis 18:25

believe Yah to be who He says is. Throughout Scripture, Yahuah invites us to inquire of Him, calls Himself our Father, and assures us of His goodness. With that in mind, why should we be afraid to ask Him anything? Sure, we may need to brace ourselves; He might humble us like He did Job or let us know it's not our business. But even then, there's no reason to fear asking.

Fear can be very loud causing us to distort the voice of the Most High. We pray about things and say we have peace. However, what we really have is peace in the familiarity of what has worked in the past. One thing we should never do is inquire of the Father when we already have our mind made up and are unwilling to change despite what we hear from Him. This is dangerous because it is fear coupled with stubbornness which are two attributes that displease Him.

I recall a sister in the faith pointing out that Yah knows His worth. This is why He is merciful but if we do not want to be right with Him, He is, indeed, willing to let us go. Although His love for us is strong, anyone with a spirit of humility can attest to the fact that He is the prize. Therefore, He knows the value of His words. Why would He waste them on a fearful, stubborn individual who is set on doing what they believe to be best? We can't claim to know how the Most High will respond in every situation because Scripture indeed says that He will have mercy on whom He chooses.[65] I wouldn't gamble on coming into His presence with this attitude because there is a very good chance that our fear will speak to us and we will confuse it with the voice of Yah. And then what? Not only will we have convinced ourselves, but we will have left no room

---

[65] Romans 9:15

for anyone else to come along and correct us because we would have already declared *"God told me!"* thus settling the matter.

Looking back, few moments illustrate fear overshadowing the voice of Yah more vividly than the response to the COVID-19 *plandemic.* Countless Believers claimed to have been led by the Holy Spirit to take the vaccine or at minimum, they claimed to have peace after praying about it. However, what they actually had peace about is their earlier experiences with pharmaceuticals, their perceived effectiveness of vaccinations, trust in healthcare officials, and safety in numbers. Surely, the world governments *wouldn't* poison their own people in mass, right?

Further examples include the fear of dying alone, causing some to enter marriage covenants with spouses that the Most High would not choose for them. Others rush to have children, regardless of circumstances, to beat their *biological clock.* While all these situations have their own set of consequences, the fact remains that the decisions we make will undoubtedly affect our relationship with Yah. Again, it is a direct reflection of how we view Him and how well we know Him. So, the question resurfaces, how can we have *intimacy with the Most High* if we allow fear to stand in the way of truly knowing Him? Later, we'll explore practical ways to live Spirit-led lives, rooted in faith, not driven by fear.

CHAPTER 8

Worldly Mindset

xperienced and *sophisticated* were the words that came up in my initial query for the definition of **worldly**. I find this particularly ironic considering who the Scriptures refer to as the god of this world.[66] If you grew up in church, or at the very least found yourself in the vicinity of Christian elders, you would be familiar with the negative connotation that the word carries. Among Believers, ***worldly*** refers to ideas, speech, and behavior that aligns with culture rather than the kingdom of Elohiym. Worldly ideologies are often in direct opposition to Biblical principles.

As mentioned previously, the mixture of that which is holy and that which is profane has made it difficult to differentiate between the two. Without the indwelling of the Holy Spirit, who gives us *eyes to see,* it is nearly impossible. Worldliness can flourish subtly within the gray areas, and in ways that seem right and morally sound according to human reasonability. However, humans are not the authority on what is righteous and just. This is where many of us struggle, and when it's addressed, it's typically met with excuses or accusations of legalism and judgment.

What we tend to underestimate is the insidiousness of the evil one. Music promoting violence, sexual immorality, and the worship of material things is easily identifiable as worldly. Overly revealing clothing, leaving little to the imagination is a no-brainer. But what about our beloved old school R&B love songs with sweet metaphors

---

[66] 2 Corinthians 4:4

reminiscent of Song of Solomon? Or what about women that wear pants? We love to play the what about-ism game, spending time and energy arguing over whether it's okay to drink wine, listen to Luther Vandross or if "godly" women should be seen in anything other than dresses and skirts.

This is low-hanging fruit, a distraction from the deeper issue: an unrenewed mind. When our minds aren't transformed, we begin to prioritize money over intangible values such as time. Entertainment over the Word of the Most High. Pride over humility. Status over obscurity. Selfishness over responsibility. Vulgarity over discretion. The constant desire for more rather than contentment. Cultural, political, and religious agendas over biblical commandments. Of course, these mindsets can show up in how we present outwardly or what we are willing to allow through our ear and eye gates, but I challenge us to consider that they are much more indicative of our spirit man and where his allegiance lies.

If there is one thing that I wish had been explained to me as a youth pursuing a relationship with my Elohiym, it is that change comes from the inside. Often, we attempt, using our own will power, to stop cursing, sleeping around, listening to trashy music, abusing substances, and so on. The fact of the matter is that some people have stronger will power than others. It is nothing more than that. Perhaps they don't have access to sexual partners or even the slightest tolerance for alcohol. Neither will power nor lack of accessibility equates to holiness. In many cases, we are simply suppressing our carnal desires, but it would only take the right circumstances to expose us. Change comes from a mind that has decided to surrender itself in totality to the Most High.

Not too long ago, I recall watching an episode of the Golden Bachelor. The main character was a widower in his seventies who took part in the show to find a new wife. He was courting a group of about 25 women, all around 60 years and older, which included a mix of ethnicities, body types, and personalities. What immediately stood out to me during the initial introductions was that the Black women seemed to be the first to broach the topic of sex and intimacy. I was instantly offended due to my observation of Black women often being over-sexualized. In fairness, some of this is of our own doing, and although I believe it to be a self-fulfilling prophecy, I digress.

In my frustration, I complained to a friend thinking she would agree with me, but she actually felt the opposite. She stated that after a certain age, Black women are no longer seen as sexual. Although it still bothered me, I had to admit that there was some truth to what she was saying. But later on I thought to myself, why would a group of women who were placed on this earth to be influencers of holiness and righteousness need to appear as sexy to anyone outside of their spouses? By no means am I insinuating that women should let themselves go and no longer put effort into their appearance. In fact, I noticed that many women on the show appeared to have been diligent in taking care of themselves. They were dressed with elegance and style, exuding a timeless class that caught the Golden Bachelor's attention, without relying on sexual innuendos. Yet, let society tell it everyone must be sexy all the time.

This is an example of a worldly mindset. The scenario starts with a half truth that Black women are often no longer seen as sexual beings after a certain age. Nevertheless, when we dig deeper, we discover that, whether it's true or not, it is irrelevant to the life of a Believer, thus exposing the distraction. The truth of the matter is that it is acceptable for a woman of any age to engage in sexual intimacy with her spouse. What does it matter if she appears *sexy* or not to someone she's not married to? The enemy loves to get us asking the wrong questions to keep our attention off the right thing. In our rush to prove that women can be sexy at any age, we often drift from the position the Most High has called us to occupy: women who honor their temples inwardly and outwardly, walk in wisdom, holiness, grace and the fruit of the Spirit[67]. Women who, according to Titus 2, instruct young ladies in the way of modesty, respect, marriage and family life.

Another example of a worldly mindset is when Roe vs Wade was overturned giving individual states the right to ban abortion. I recall getting an extremely long text rant from someone about how wrong this was. I was perplexed as this individual was in her 40s, desired to have children, and identified as a Christian. For the life of me, I could not understand how this applied to her in any way. But again, this is what the enemy does. He gets us so riled up about **women's rights** that we don't realize that what we are trying to align ourselves with is not of the Most High.

I'm using women in these scenarios because that is what I know and with whom I'm typically in close fellowship with. Worldliness tends to show up in men as it relates to their attitudes regarding sex, money, and even finding their identity in what they *do* rather than in the Most High. Black men, and any man that calls himself a follower of the Messiah, are called to be the priests of their homes; sexually chaste, preservers of their precious seed. They are called to be leaders, teachers, and models of righteousness according to how Scripture defines it. I recently heard someone say, *"a man lacking purpose distracts himself with pleasure."* I concur, being that the pleasures of this world are given at liberty by the god of this world.

---

[67] Galatians 5:22-23

Ultimately, worldliness is a mindset that shapes our morals, values, and preferences based on man's standards. A religious mindset can also be worldly because it is man's idea of how to worship the Most High instead of how He has instructed us to.

How Worldliness Hinders

A worldly mindset hinders our intimacy with the Father because it distorts the way we approach relationship with Him. We often A) expect it to mirror our human relationships, and B) lose patience far quicker than we would if we were pursuing a romantic connection or nurturing a close friendship. This is due to our lack of reverence fueled by inadequate knowledge of who He is. In His Word, He tells us that His thoughts and ways are higher than ours.[68] There are also several Scriptures throughout the Bible that teach us that we must wait on the Most High. Lamentations 3:25 is one of many.

Comfort, convenience, and instant gratification are top priorities in this society. When we take a step back to look at the push for everything to be faster and smarter, it can be a bit unnerving. As humans, we can only achieve so much, hence the integration of technology. It has gone from desktop computers, to laptops, to smart phones, to smart watches. Now, since getting our info with a flick of the wrist is too much effort, the next phase appears to be having a mechanism implanted into the palm of our hand.

Social media has left us unnaturally overstimulated which no doubt has affected our brain functionality. I was an avid reader as a child and young adult but currently, I find it more difficult to read books. My flesh would rather scroll, having my mind constantly

---

[68] Isaiah 58:8-9

inundated with a variety of topics along with the latest information. When there is an online article, I scroll down first to see how long it is before I commit to reading the entire thing. On YouTube, there are instances when I visit the comment section first to see if the video is worth my time. Technology, social media, and the overall culture of convenience has not only done a number on our collective attention spans, but it has also conditioned our minds in ways that breed laziness, impatience, and entitlement.

Unfortunately, if we are not mindful, these traits will have an adverse effect on our relationship with the Most High especially if we do not understand how He interacts with us. For instance, while I may have my own personal struggles, I do understand that Scripture is the best way for me to get to know Him, understand His expectations of me, and nurture our relationship.

Therefore, attention span issues and all, reading the Word of Yah is a non-negotiable for me. For those who are new to their faith journey in an advanced technological era, the challenge can feel that much more daunting. This is why a renewing of the mind is paramount as it's important to understand what our priorities are. Is it politics, the news, sports, pop-culture, or the Word of our Creator? At some point, we will have to decide and act on it. We have all heard the saying that "love is a choice". Our relationship with Yah is no different. Everyday we must guard against laziness and distraction to ensure that He receives our attention and adoration. Will we fall short at times? Absolutely, just as we are not always the perfect spouse, parent, or friend. However, being that our Heavenly Father is the prize above all, our efforts should be that much greater.

Impatience is a major hindrance as we often do not understand that it is His expectation that we wait on Him. In my experience with the Most High, I have learned that He always answers me.

Often, the answer is not immediate. I have learned to trust His reasons for that as there is a time and a season for everything. There is also a way in which He may prefer to deliver the answer. This may come through Scripture, another person, or situation. If I approach our relationship with the same expectation that it will always be a quick back and forth exchange like I would have with a human, then not only have I set myself up for disappointment, but I have also held Elohiym to *my* standards instead of submitting to His. This is not to say that a conversational exchange is not possible. In fact, I believe that is often something that blossoms with time as our ears become fine tuned to discern His voice.

The rapidly growing sense of entitlement that we are experiencing in our culture can also rear its ugly head in our relationship with Yah. After years of ignoring our Creator and going our own way, we finally decide to give him 5-10 minutes of our day. We then give up after a week when we perceive that nothing has changed. A worldly mindset says that because I showed up and did the bare minimum, there should be some type of reward. The Most High says that He is a rewarder to those that diligently seek Him[69]. He also says that when we ask for things, we ask amiss which in a nutshell means that we are praying with a worldly mindset[70]. These prayers are often selfish, shallow, and not aligned or submitted to the will of Yah. I cannot emphasize enough how important it is that we ask Him to help us see things from His perspective rather than our own.

A worldly mindset makes it difficult for Yah to communicate with us because our minds are filled with carnal knowledge rather than the Word which edifies our spirit man. It creates a language

---

[69] Hebrews 11:6

[70] James 4:3

barrier. He speaks in terms of holistic prosperity, while we're often preoccupied with things that moths can destroy, rust can decay, or thieves can steal.[71] We also like to skip the sanctification process for what we're requesting and go straight for the gold. We ask for a huge new home without even the thought of making it a house of prayer or a place where people can seek temporary shelter if needed.

Worldliness robs us of an intimate relationship with Yah because our focus is not where it should be. Again, there is nothing wrong with being informed of the things going on around us, but that is different from it being our priority. Overly centering ourselves on worldly matters can scramble our moral compass. It invites confusion, particularly if we do not have a strong spiritual foundation. Whatever or whomever we put our heart, mind, soul, and strength on becomes our god. When we do not take **being in the world but not of it** to heart, we become hyper aware and concerned about how the world views us.[72] We tend to care more about what people think rather than being *peculiar.*[73] Yahuah says that friendship with the world is enmity with Him. We cannot have intimacy with someone that we have enmity with.

Most importantly, we must understand that none of this is coincidental. As mentioned before, the enemy plays the long game and knows exactly how his worldly trinkets will affect us, be it technology, world events, entertainment, etc. I am not calling any of these things inherently wicked as they all have a place in today's world. This just means that we must remain mindful of how the enemy mixes good with evil to distract us. Moreover, we must be

---

[71] Matthew 6:19-20

[72] John 15:19

[73] Deuteronomy 14:2

vigilant to maintain a heart posture that esteems an intimate relationship with the Most High above all else.

Unforgiveness & Resentment

Years ago, a failed relationship left me extremely hurt and resentful. It was a dark period in my life, in general, and I was in a lot of pain. One particular late night, while driving through the Phoenix desert I found myself listening to Dr. Charles Stanley on satellite radio. He was speaking on unforgiveness and I quickly realized that this is what I was dealing with. Until that point, I had not consciously dealt with much unforgiveness. This caught me off guard and I realized that I was in uncharted territory. It also became immediately clear that I had confused the "the time heals all wounds" concept with forgiveness. I had been unconsciously waiting for the pain to subside as an indication that I had forgiven this person.

Dr. Stanley made me realize that this was something that I needed to consciously do. Furthermore, as cliche as it sounds, I also learned that I needed to forgive for my own benefit. Once I released the bitterness and resentment I was holding towards this individual, a weight was lifted off of me. This doesn't mean that there weren't still hurt feelings or disappointment but I no longer had negative feelings toward this person. It was a powerful and liberating lesson.

I've had a bit more practice since then and I must admit that each time caught me by surprise as it's not really my nature to hold a grudge. When someone genuinely apologizes or makes an effort at reconciliation it's almost impossible for me to stay angry. The challenge came when there was no acknowledgement of any wrongdoing let alone an apology. I realized that I was holding something against someone from years ago and was honestly too embarrassed to even bring it up, especially since it had no material effect on my life. Nevertheless, once I became aware that I was holding something against a friend, I decided to ask the Most High to help me move on from that. I also noticed that my lack of forgiveness was preventing me from seeing the growth and maturity in this individual because I was still viewing them in light of the incident from long ago.

As with most of the other hindrances that we have discussed, unforgiveness is often perpetuated by a faulty perspective. We neglect to consider how much Yah has forgiven us for including the crucifixion of the Messiah who He sent to restore us back to Him. From the Garden of Eden until present day, our list of offenses is long. In fact, it is almost certain that we often offend the Most High out of ignorance. Yet, that does not prevent Him from waking us up, providing for us, and protecting us throughout the day. This should help us to realize that we are in no position to withhold forgiveness from anyone. Actually, it is quite audacious as it is safe to say that none of us have sinned against another human being more than we've sinned against our Elohiym. As sobering as that thought is, it is a necessary one to keep us in check when we struggle with finding another person worthy of grace.

From a scriptural standpoint, we understand that confession and repentance are all necessary components when seeking forgiveness. Typically, we only view these when pertaining to our relationship with the Father. However, I would venture to say that these apply to our relationships with our brothers and sisters as well. The Bible also adds instructions for restitution where applicable. Nowhere in Scripture can I find that we are required to forgive someone that is unrepentant towards us. However, Yah knows our hearts, and He has placed a safeguard against loopholes by commanding us to go to our brother or sister if we have an issue with them. So, for those of us who like to stay mad, and think we're let off the hook because the person never came to us, we would still be considered out of order.

The Scriptures give detailed instruction on how to deal with those who we believe wronged us. If none of those things work, then we are instructed to deal with them as heathens.[74] This means we are permitted to separate from them. Still, the caveat remains, that it does us well to forgive, even if not explicitly commanded as not to harbor bitterness in our hearts. There is no getting around it, forgiveness is a must even if true reconciliation of the relationship is not possible. We are required to be of pure heart so that our relationship with the Father is not hindered.

How Unforgiveness & Resentment Hinders

"For if you forgive men their trespasses, your heavenly Father will also forgive you. But if you do not forgive men their trespasses, neither will your Father forgive your trespasses."
—Matthew 6:14-15

First and foremost, it must be understood that forgiveness is not optional. It is a commandment that is directly correlated to how the Father says He will deal with us.[75] Refusing to forgive, disqualifies us from receiving the forgiveness that we desperately need from Him. Now let's think about this for a moment. We've all done things that we are not proud of, things that if given a second chance we'd do differently. Unfortunately, that's not how life works. Once it's

---

[74] Matthew 18:15-17
[75] Matthew 18:35

done, it's done. Once the words come out of our mouths, there is no taking them back.

Now, imagine having done something that you genuinely regret and have no intention of repeating. You sorrowfully go to the Father to apologize and make amends, and He tells you that He doesn't forgive you. Not only is that a depressing thought but it is also terrifying. If Yah does not forgive you then you will spend eternity apart from Him. I know hell isn't a popular subject these days but it's still a real place. The truth doesn't cease to be true because we deny it or refuse to speak on it.

This scenario goes hand in hand with the ***"depart from me"*** Scripture. There, the Messiah is telling people to depart from Him because He doesn't know them.[76] This means there is no intimate relationship and He regards them as strangers. Only strangers will be unforgiven so do not go in the way of such. We must imitate our Heavenly Father in forgiveness so that our path to His heart remains unobstructed.

Resentment is the part of unforgiveness that has us constantly replaying how we were wronged. The word broken down means re (again) sen (feel or sense). Allowing resentment to fester can lead to mental illness and in some cases, it can manifest as sickness in our physical bodies. Anyone dealing with mental health issues, even in temporary cases such as situational depression, can attest to how difficult it is to connect with the Most High during these times. By nature, we want to self soothe with anything that will give even a brief reprieve from the pain. Furthermore, let's consider how our brains are increasingly programmed for quick fixes and intolerant of any inconvenience. This generation is severely lacking in coping

---

[76] Matthew 7:21-23

skills. Even those of us who know to wait on the Most High struggle in this area. Therefore, none of us can afford to allow resentment to become a stronghold in our lives making us sick while simultaneously creating a barrier for us to seek out our Divine Physician.

Unforgiveness and resentment can also be a hindrance because it's not always other people that we harbor these feelings toward, but rather the Most High Himself. We are quick to blame Him for everything, including our own decisions (that we didn't include Him in) which often leads to chaos. If we're honest, we certainly have to admit one thing: while the Most High is not always the originator of everything that happens to us, He is sovereign. He either causes or allows. This can be difficult to reconcile especially in terms of weightier matters such as loss or chronic illness.

Again, perspective is key. Many of us have unrealistic expectations of what life on earth should be like. We ignore what the Scriptures teach us about living in a broken and sinful world and become irate with Yah when bad things happen. He was still good when bad things were happening to someone else but when it's us, His character is called into question. Now we're no longer sure if we can trust Him and find ourselves in the midst of a faith crisis. A place where there is no sickness, poverty, violence, or death is called Heaven. Our job on earth is to be tried and found worthy of living there with our Elohiym forever. Once we put away our entitlement and rose-colored glasses, we are in a better position to allow our trials and tribulations to draw us nearer to the Father rather than push us away. It is then that we can understand that every hardship is an opportunity to be refined like gold while experiencing His loving care.

We each respond differently to pain. Some are quick to throw themselves at His feet for mercy while others attempt to shut Him out. Nevertheless, it is much easier to embrace Him in the midst of adversity when we already have a close relationship with Him. This is why it's important to seek Yah during the *good times* so that when the storms come, we have already been fortified by His love and remain keenly aware of where our help comes from. I pray that none of us will allow unforgiveness or resentment to impede the most important relationship that we will ever have.

CHAPTER 10

Idolatry

An entire collection of books could be composed to cover the subject of idolatry. Oh wait! Several books *have* been written about man choosing any and everything over his Elohiym. Beginning with Genesis, we have Eve who puts more trust in what the serpent says rather than the instructions of the Creator.[77] We then see Adam placing his wife's desires over his Creator's.[78] At the end of this compilation, we find ourselves in Revelation. Here it is prophesied that in future times, men will choose the mark of the beast to preserve their lives on earth in exchange for eternity with their Creator.[79] In between these points, we find golden calves, gods made of wood and stone, mammon, celebrities, and so on.

Recall the recurring theme we have explored: the subtle blending of good and evil, discernible only to eyes trained by the Holy Spirit. Modern idols are no exception. They often manifest as seemingly good and commonplace aspects of life such as marriage, children, pets, careers, church activities, sports, food, social media, and even beauty routines. What does hair and makeup have to do with idolatry, one might ask. Consider the time, effort, and resources we invest in these areas. Now, contrast that with the attention we devote to nurturing our relationship with Yah. When our priorities shift away from Him, anything can become an idol.

---

[77] Genesis 3:1-13

[78] Genesis 3:17

[79] Revelation 13

Ignorance regarding idolatry prevails because we do not fully understand worship. Worship is often thought of as raising our hands and singing praises. While this is a part of it, an online dictionary expounds on this definition by adding the words ***extravagant respect, honor,*** or ***devotion.*** Are there instances where respect and devotion are appropriate? Absolutely. Scripture gives instruction on how to properly honor one another. Nevertheless, if we are collectively giving anything more of our heart, mind, soul, and strength than the Most High, then that is what we are indeed worshiping. These are not just words. Take a moment to reflect on what you have a deep affinity for. What is your mind preoccupied with? How does it play out in your actions via your will? How much effort are you putting into this person or pursuit?

I would imagine that the list of modern-day idols may have triggered some readers. Rather than taking offense let it be an opportunity for examination, followed by repentance and growth where applicable. We can begin by dissecting Mark 12:30 which reads: ***"And you shall love Yahuah Elohayka with all your heart, and with all your soul, and with all your mind, and with all your strength: this is the first commandment."***

Yahusha's instructions on loving our Elohiym serve as a framework for self-examination, helping us identify and guard against idolatry.[80] We will use work as our control factor in the following example. On a daily basis, we typically spend more concentrated time at work than we do with the Most High. The Father understands this, which is why He has given us six days to work and one day to rest in Him. It is important to understand that time does not always equate to effort.

---

[80] Matthew 22:37

So, let's begin by considering the *heart* section of the equation. Do we care more about our status on this job than our position in the Kingdom? If Yah asked us to give it up, how difficult would it be? Next, is the *mind*. When we are at work, do we think of our Elohiym? Do we acknowledge, or include Him in our decision making? When we're not working, do thoughts of work consume us more than our thoughts of Him? Consider the *soul* which includes emotions that ultimately produce action; do we find it difficult not to work on the day that He commanded us to rest in Him? When we do, are we trying to rush through worship so that we can have the rest of the day "free"? Lastly, we have *strength* which can be measured in the form of effort. How does the intensity of how we work our jobs compare with the passion in which we nurture our relationship with the Most High? This exercise can be used to evaluate a number of areas in our lives. It's as simple as identifying our strongest desires and being honest with how we interact with them in comparison to our relationship with our Heavenly Father.

There is one idol intentionally left off the list. It is arguably the most pervasive one of today, glaringly displayed online through social media profiles as well as narcissistic tendencies in person. It is the idol of self. This includes everything from shameless self centering all the way to self identification. We did not create ourselves, the earth, nor did we establish order. Yet, we assume to have the authority to define who and what we are on an intrinsic level. *Self* has been so elevated that we have made the Creator into our own image. This image thrives in individualistic rhetoric where we all do what seems right in our own eyes. We have drifted so far from the Divine moral compass that basic understanding, such as the creation of male and female, has become a convoluted matter requiring government intervention.

The image of self allows us to dictate everything from natural order to day-to-day righteousness. Some even get crafty and use the term **universe** in place of *God*. We expose ourselves by the fact that we would prefer to deal with a created thing, the universe, instead of the One who created it. Now why would that be the case? I've heard people speak of how the universe leads, guides, and provides but I have never heard anyone say that the universe challenged them or held them accountable for any wrongdoing. The universe is a vague unstructured *god* whose ways seem to always coincide with our own will. This mindset seeks to obtain all the things we feel entitled to without any accountability. At best, the *universe* we appeal to is merely an echo of our own desires; at worst, it becomes the deceptive voice of the enemy leading us astray.

When it comes to idolatry, we often miss the point that the Most High expects loyalty. Perhaps if we began looking at it from this perspective it would be more relatable. For instance, consider this story from my youth: Decades ago, when I was barely old enough to legally order a glass of wine, I found myself in a relationship with someone that I had every intention of marrying. In retrospect, we had no business being in this type of intimate arrangement that was meant for marriage. Nevertheless, there was still an agreed upon expectation of exclusivity.

Well, after some time, I received the shock of my 20 something year old life, when I discovered that my boyfriend had been secretly involved in a relationship with another young woman. Confused and heartbroken, I immediately broke up with him. Now, although we were young, we genuinely cared for one another so when he begged me to take him back, I obliged. Re-entering the relationship, it became painfully clear that the trust was broken, and things were not the same.

However, we were mature enough to know that the relationship was redeemable if that was what we both wanted and were willing to work at it. When the relationship eventually ended it was not due to lack of trust or because I caught him cheating again. I broke up with him because one day I came to visit him, and he was wearing a t-shirt from a church that his little side girlfriend attended. I was furious and demanded that he take it off. He refused and I promptly broke up with him. For good. It may seem petty, and we can laugh about it now, but all I can say is I am my Father's child. He said He will not be mocked[81] and neither will I.

Let's put this into the context of our relationship with our Creator. Yes, the perfect One who sits outside of time, but took the time to create a beautiful earth for us to inhabit. He made us in His image, placed His life giving breath into us, and throughout the course of our lives, protects, provides, and interacts with us. If that's not enough, when we fell short of His standards, causing a great divide between us, He left glory and both literally and figuratively lowered Himself to our level. He provided an example of how we were to live before allowing His own creation to torture and kill Him, all as a way of reconciling us back to Him. If that is not one who is worthy of complete loyalty and devotion, then I don't know who is.

The fact remains that we have all been caught being unfaithful to Yah at some point. At one time or another we've placed our own desires above His will. Being the patient Father that He is, when we seek forgiveness and exhibit true repentance, He gladly welcomes us back.

---

[81] Galatians 6:7

Nonetheless, He expects us to make a clean break from our "lover". There is no flirting, winking, keeping the hoodie that smells like them, remaining friends, or occasionally keeping in touch. Yah says that He is a jealous Elohiym[82] and considers our unfaithfulness to be whoredom.[83] Of course there are times when we simply need to re-prioritize. Obviously, we wouldn't just put away our spouse, kids, or jobs. This is also not meant to condemn anyone for enjoying sports or putting effort into their appearance. These things can be partaken of in a balanced way that do not rival our devotion to our Creator.

However, when it comes to idol worship in the spiritual sense, we must take heed. This is why a growing number of Believers are so adamantly against pagan holidays. Where in Scripture did the Most High tell the Israelites that they could keep the idol (i.e., Christmas tree)[84] as long as they didn't worship it? Nowhere! There are numerous verses where Yahuah tells His people to smash, destroy, and burn the idols altogether. Who would want a reminder of their spouse's indiscretion just laying around as a constant reminder? What's puzzling is the fact that many Believers know that these holidays are rooted in pagan worship. And who do pagans serve if there is only one true living Elohiym? Who is the father of all lies? Who is the god of this world? Who said, "I will ascend above the tops of the clouds; I will make myself like the Most High?"[85] Who is at the top of this progressive beast system that will ultimately result in people openly worshiping him? It is none other than Santa himself. I mean satan.

---

[82] Exodus 20:5

[83] Hosea 4:12

[84] Jeremiah 10:1-5

[85] Isaiah 14:14

These things matter. If they didn't, why were the Israelites always being judged due to idol worship? Why is it the very first commandment, backed by the second?[86] Why is it included in the summary of the law given by Messiah? Even Paul, not wanting to burden the gentiles with all the intricacies of Torah, at minimum warned them against eating food sacrificed to idols.[87] The Scripture says that there was a time that Elohiym winked at our ignorance[88] but now some of us are walking in shameless rebellion because we care more about our traditions than the commandments of Yahuah.[89] It mattered to the Most High then and it matters today.

How Idolatry Hinders

We serve an emotional Elohiym. If you don't believe so, read the book of Jeremiah. My prayer partner and I have been brought to tears listening to the Creator of the universe express anguish at His people's betrayal. At one point it seems as if He's actually questioning Himself as to what He's done wrong to make Israel be so unfaithful.[90] If you've ever been betrayed in a relationship you know the feeling of second guessing yourself all too well. Idolatry hinders our relationship with Yahuah because it hurts His feelings. We are not to just have fire insurance when it comes to our Creator. He desires an emotional connection with us. How is this possible when idols that don't hold a candle to Him are positioned on the thrones of our hearts?

Idols are so deceptive because they provide the illusion that they will satisfy us. We intuitively believe that a family, money, or the

---

[86] Exodus 20:3-4
[87] Acts 15:19-20
[88] Acts 17:30
[89] Mark 7:7-13
[90] Jeremiah 2:5

perfect career will bring the contentment that our soul longs for. When it does not, we're left confused. Even worse is when total fulfillment is found in those things making it nearly impossible to recognize our need for a Savior, leaving us to die in our sins. Scripture talks about how difficult it is for a rich man to enter the Kingdom of Yah[91]. We should consider it a mercy of the Most High when we are unable to find true contentment apart from Him.

Even those that 'have it all' but still feel empty, will still refuse to tap into their spirit man to connect with their Creator. Instead, they go harder, longer, and stronger for the idol believing that once they get to the next level they will be satisfied. It may seem like all of our hard work at the job, to the neglect of our spirit man is profitable, but that is delusional thinking. It is yet another trick of the enemy used to consume our time and energy so we have little left to offer the Most High. In fact, the set-up of this world system is purposely orchestrated to keep us too distracted or exhausted to nurture our relationship with our Creator. It is designed to steal our time, energy, resources and ultimately our lives.

We must remain discerning even in the midst of things that seem ordinary and good, bearing in mind the intentionality of the god of this world and the fact that he is ultimately Yah's enemy. His aim is to get us to serve him directly but he will settle for deceiving us into doing it indirectly. It doesn't matter to him as long as we aren't serving the Most High. Yahusha explicitly said that we cannot serve two masters.[92] Therefore, as long as we have idols, then our relationship with Him will be hindered.

---

[91] Matthew 19:21-23
[92] Matthew 6:24

The further danger in idolatry is that it has the capacity to completely destroy us: mentally, emotionally, financially, physically and even spiritually. Think about how mad we drive ourselves when we become consumed with something that is out of our reach. We exhaust all of our time and resources trying to obtain it and, when we don't, intrusive dark thoughts cause us to question if life is even worth it. Being distraught by what we can't have to the point of hopeless despair is a form of torment that can lead to mental illness. As we've discussed before, it can be very difficult to interact with the Most High when we are physically or mentally unwell. It is our responsibility to be vigilant in keeping our hearts pure from anything that could pose a threat to our connection with our Elohiym.

Similarly to pride, idolatry also drives a wedge between us and the Most High because idols make it difficult to properly hear the voice of the Holy Spirit. We can be so consumed by what we want that it begins to dictate how we believe we are being led. Again, the Most High competes with the voice of no one, including our idols.

Not to bring up old stuff, but we can look back to the 2020 elections for a clear example of this. We had so many voices claiming to hear from "God" that Donald Trump was going to win the election. What was clear to me is that these individuals viewed Christian conservative ideals and biblical principles as one and the same. They had put so much faith in a political party, and its leader, that they could not fathom how the country would withstand if their savior was not elected into office. The Democrats possessed the same thought process, which ironically, is on full display now in 2025 with the loss of their candidate. Nevertheless, back then there were Believers that needed Donald Trump to be President so badly that they began to declare that God had actually told them that he would win.

At this time, I was spiritually discerning enough to know that we had already reached a point where it didn't matter who the president-elect was. End times events will play out regardless of who is wearing the face of the presidency. Back then, I was still relatively new in terms of prophetic understanding. Therefore, although I didn't have a dog in the fight, I believed the *prophets* who were saying that Trump was going to win. For me it was the sheer amount of people, who as far as I knew were genuine Believers, that were stating this claim. It went from self proclaimed prophets to simple laymen who claimed to be able to hear the voice of God. I didn't understand how all of these people, who were so boldly adamant, could be wrong. So I shrugged my shoulders and said well I guess that's what it will be. Imagine my confusion when it was announced that Joe Biden had indeed been elected. Red flags started flying up like possessed whack-a-moles and claiming a stolen election (whether true or false) was not going to account for the fact that someone had lied and it wasn't the Most High!

A couple of weeks later, I received my answer. I was in bed listening to one of my favorite prophetic voices at the time. On his podcast, he was actually interviewing another prophet and they were speaking of the elections and how so many so-called prophets had been proven to be false. What the interviewee said next caused me to sit straight up in bed. Citing Ezekiel 14, specifically verse 9, she said that they were deceived because, due to their idolatry, the Most High, Himself, had deceived these people. This is also what the Scripture says verbatim. I don't know how long I sat there with my mouth open but it all made sense. Whether these people were idolizing Trump himself, the Republican party, or holding tight to

Christian Nationalism which depends on the preservation of America, somewhere their faith had been placed in something or someone other than their Elohiym and this was the end result.

I would encourage anyone to stop and take the time to read Ezekiel Chapter 14 for yourself. This is Yahuah speaking directly about how He deals with those who harbor idolatry in their hearts. It is a serious barrier to our communication with Him which is a full proof way to invite deception and confusion. Idolatry is clothed in a thick cloud of hurt; we hurt the Most High, we hurt ourselves, and we can hurt one another by being a vessel in which chaos infiltrates the body of Mashiach. In essence, idolatry violates the greatest commandments given by the Messiah, to love our Elohiym, with all our hearts, souls, minds and to love our neighbors as ourselves.

PART III

Increasing Intimacy with the Most High

Introduction to Increasing Intimacy with the Most High

In Part II, we have gone over what not to do, but simply *not doing* does not guarantee spiritual elevation. It's like one who abstains from food but never incorporates prayer into their time of fasting. Sure, the body may be healthier but there has been no change to the soul. Similarly, when we stay clear of certain sins, our relationships with one another improve and we enjoy an overall better quality of life. This is because Yahuah's principles and laws are universal. This is also why satan is able to lead people to confuse prosperity with righteousness. We've all heard people boast that they must be doing something right because they are being blessed. Well, as Elohiym's creations we are all provided a general measure of grace. Yahuah makes His sun rise on the evil and on the good. He sends rain on the just and the unjust. [93]

The Scriptures also teach us that satan has the ability to bless people as well. Remember when he tried to convince Yahusha to worship him in exchange for all the kingdoms of the world? [94] Revelation 3:17 talks about how the riches of those in need of nothing can blind them to their true spiritual state. For instance, we have entertainers who put out some of the most vile, degrading, and demonic content but are quick to thank *God* for their success. We have to wonder which god?

---

[93] Matthew 5:45
[94] Matthew 4:9

If you truly want to know and become intimate with the One True Living Elohiym as introduced to us through our Hebrew ancestors, the One who created the heavens, Earth, everything in between, the One who knows all, sees all, and has all power in His hands, the One who is infinitely intelligent, creative, wise and still has the nerve to be the most loving Being that has ever existed, if you believe that pursuit to be worth your life, then stay with me as we move to Part 3 of this book. There we will discuss actionable steps, to remove the hindrances and take you closer to experience the true fulfillment that an intimate relationship with our Elohiym promises.

CHAPTER 11

Repentance

The hindrances that we discussed in Part 2 all fall into the category of sin, but it is imperative to know that despite what is commonly taught, all sin is NOT equal. "All sin is sin" is an often-parroted phrase for which there is no scriptural support. Contrarily, 1 John 5:16 refers to sin that does not lead to death. Matthew 12:31 speaks of blasphemy of the Holy Spirit being an unforgivable sin. We also have instances of Yahuah making comparisons between Israel and Judah, as well as other nations, in regard to their sin.[95] From these verses we can ascertain that the Most High, the Righteous Judge, does indeed make a distinction between sins. *"No sin is greater than the other"* is a lie meant to subtly discourage us from pursuing righteousness. If speeding by a mile, a violation of the laws of the land[96], is equivalent to adultery, then an evil heart would argue that our actions don't truly matter because God sees everything equally. This belief is further reinforced by the false notion that all we need to do is ask for forgiveness, which is different from genuine repentance.

Interestingly enough, my sister and I recently had a conversation about this very thing. She agreed with me and said, yes because covetousness is not the same as committing murder. While she is correct, covetousness is still a murderous spirit that can result in actual murder if fully manifested. We see an example of this in the story of King David who coveted Bathsheba, eventually leading to

---

[95] Jeremiah 3:10-11, Ezekial 16:48-51
[96] Romans 13:1-7

the death of her husband.[97] By no means is this an attempt to create a hierarchy of sin. We should not be giving the enemy so much as a foothold as we march towards the mark of perfection. Nonetheless, this writing is not about sinning and not sinning. It may simply appear that way because that is often what stands in the way of our relationship with our Creator.

This book is for those who have either put away the *sins of the flesh* or who are actively on the path to do so. Galatians 5:19-21 refers to these as: adultery, fornication, uncleanness, lewdness, idolatry, sorcery, hatred, contentions, jealousies, outbursts of wrath, selfish ambitions, dissensions, heresies, envy, murders, drunkenness, revelries, and the like. The Most High will not be mocked so if we think that we can intentionally and persistently partake in these things and still have intimacy with Him, we are deceiving ourselves. Many of us are so preoccupied with trying to stop fornicating, stop abusing substances, or even fighting amongst ourselves to prove that our *doctrine* is right that we do not make way for the deeper things of Yah. The constant struggle becomes a distraction in itself, as a religious spirit suggests that overcoming these sins is the ultimate goal.

Yet overcoming sin is not the end goal. Our main objective is becoming one with our Creator. To be one with Him means we must be holy as He is holy. Becoming one is the height of intimacy and putting away sin provides the foundation for it. Recall the Scripture that says that Elohiym no longer dwells within buildings made by human hands.[98] We are the temples in which He desires to dwell. He is Holy and cannot and will not be unified with a filthy vessel.[99]

---

[97] 2 Samuel 11:1-16

[98] Acts 7:48-51

[99] 2 Corinthians 6:16-17

We must be vigilant in our understanding that the enemy loves to pervert the commandments of the Most High along with His intended purposes for them. Through a religious spirit, he implies that once we've overcome the flesh, we will have reached a new level of spirituality. Actually, it is reaching a new level of spirituality that breaks us free from the bondage of sin. This leads us to our first action step which is rooted in the power of choice. Many of us still struggle because we have not made a determined decision in our minds to live righteously. In essence, we have not fully repented. We have made promises to stop doing one thing while still doing another. Yet, the focus should not be on doing or not doing. It is our mindset that needs a radical paradigm shift. We must make an intentional, decisive choice to completely surrender our will to that of the Most High and allow Him to take us through the sanctification process.

Personally, it was not until I made a conscious decision to wholeheartedly follow Yah, with the help of the Holy Spirit, that I was able to let go of the works of the flesh and allow Him to work on the hidden aspects of my heart. It was as if once the "big" sins were done away with it was time to get to the root of things. For me that included pride, unforgiveness/resentment, worldliness, etc. In full transparency, I had no idea that there was so much inner work that needed to be done.

Over the years I had met few Believers who lived by the principles of holiness as prescribed by Scripture. While the church referenced big sins from time to time the emphasis seemed to be on asking for forgiveness and having the certainty that we were forgiven through the shed blood of Christ. The churches that I attended later focused on *being like Jesus* to the tune of fostering community and loving your neighbor demonstrated by charitable works. As the culture continued to infiltrate the church, certain topics became more normalized. Eventually things such as fornication and gossip were presented as more of a suggestion rather than distinguishing factors in living a set apart life. Furthermore, homosexuality and gluttony were rarely addressed.

These selective tiers of acceptable behavior subtly set the table for the standard to become our fellow human beings rather than the written and living Word found in the person of Yahusha Ha'Mashiach. Many believe that because they are fornicating with the opposite sex it leaves them in the clear. There are also married people who think that because they are not fornicating or committing adultery that they are living righteously. These are the bare minimum standards of a Believer that have been around since the days of Moses. Abstaining from them while not addressing pride, idolatry, worldliness, etc. will leave us in a state of confusion as to why our relationship with the Most High is stagnant. That is if we even have eyes to see that it is indeed stagnant. Regularly attending church while reciting and receiving the same talking points since 1985 is not spiritual growth. It is a breeding ground for complacency clothed in self righteousness.

I recently had a profound revelation about the Most High. By "recent," I mean I finally had the aha moment where the pieces He has been presenting to me for some time finally came together. Do we find it curious that we are never commanded to trust one another? Instead, we are encouraged to place our full trust in Elohiym. Yet those of us who subscribe to a *relationship over religion* belief system should know that relationships are reciprocal. Let me propose a second question: Would you trust someone with your secrets that has demonstrated pridefulness, selfishness, lack of self control, etc.? Of course not. If we want to truly be a friend of the

Most High, that means He must be able to trust us, too. He is an Elohiym that desires to be known and tell us great and hidden things. [100] But He is not for everyone. Better put, He is not everyone's cup of tea.

The Father invites us all, but there are certain conditions that must be met. Again, putting away the sins of the flesh is the bare minimum. Despite what has been taught, what we've heard or how we feel, John 9:31 says that the Most High does not hear the prayers of sinners. Unless, of course, it is a genuine prayer of repentance. Even as repentant Believers, the level of access that we have to our holy Creator is determined by how holy we are willing to become ourselves. Will we settle for the bare minimum, or will we allow ourselves to be refined like gold for the reward of having an intimate relationship with the Most High beyond what we thought was possible? If you are ready to make this step, I want to encourage you to pray a prayer of repentance today. It does not matter how long you have been "saved", in church, or even in leadership.

For the record, repentance is a life-long journey. It also includes things that were done by others in our bloodline. [101] Yet, it must start with us as individuals. We must come clean, with humility, and admit that we have fallen short and not gotten things right. At minimum, most of us are guilty of trusting in man's instruction on how to serve Yahuah rather than the way He has given us in Scripture.

I'm not going to offer a "sinner's prayer." I know that many may have come into faith using that, so I won't go as far as to say that it is ineffective. However, the entire premise of this book is about

---

[100] Jeremiah 33:3
[101] Leviticus 26:40-42

establishing our own personal relationship with the Father outside of religious traditions. He wants us, in our own words, to confess our wrongdoing, agree to His terms and conditions going forward, and request His help in fulfilling them. At this point, you don't have to necessarily list out every single sin that you can ever recall, unless you feel led to do so. The Holy Spirit may, indeed, lead you to a season of this during your sanctification process. For now, it's important to speak earnestly to Father about where you are presently and make your need and desire for Him known.

"All that the Father gives Me will come to Me, and the one who comes to Me I will by no means cast out." —John 6:37

If you are reading this book with the intention of having a closer relationship with your Creator, then you can be certain that the Father is calling out to you. It is your destiny to experience salvation and dwell with Him, not only in the world to come, but to experience Him right here in this lifetime. A relationship with Yahuah, made possible through the sacrifice of His Son, is a slice of Heaven on earth. Whether you prayed this prayer for salvation or elevation, I want to assure you that the best days of your life are ahead of you. May the Most High bless and keep you from this day forward!

CHAPTER 12

Authentic Relationship

Our culture is relationship obsessed. To a degree, this is understandable being that they are foundational to our societal existence. The topic is relentlessly touted in every form of media from books, podcasts, tv shows, websites, movies, blogs, to apps and so on. When we don't get answers from the comfort of our homes, we enlist the support of therapists and counselors to mediate our familial, romantic, professional, and even platonic connections.

With so much difficulty in living harmoniously with one another, it's no wonder that we struggle to maintain a thriving relationship with an unseen Elohiym. Nevertheless, the greatest commandments inform us that both are required.[102] The order in which they are given instructs us to prioritize our relationship with our Elohiym above anyone else. Yet, both in and outside of faith-based circles, the emphasis on human relationships often takes precedence.

While the Creator is distinct from His creation, majestic, and worthy of a divine reverence that is exclusive to Him, we are still able to employ some trusted relationship basics to engage with Him. In this chapter we will discuss four principles of an authentic relationship that we can put into practice to deepen our connection to our Heavenly Father. As with any relationship, effort is requisite, and time is our teacher. We will receive what we put into it. As we continue our sanctification process, we'll also grow in knowledge

---

[102] Matthew 22:36-40

and understanding of our Elohiym, thus becoming wiser and more discerning of how to interact with Him.

Principle 1: Acknowledgement & Agreement

A wedding serves as a public acknowledgement of a binding agreement that two people have made. During the ceremony, the couple recites vows, *the governing laws,* of their covenant in the presence of witnesses. When it comes to the Most High, Yah says that in order to please Him we must first acknowledge that He exists.[103] The Creator has a clear message for atheists, calling them wicked and without excuse: ***"For since the creation of the world His invisible attributes, His invisible attributes are clearly seen, being understood by the things that are made, even His eternal power and Godhead, so that they are without excuse."*** —Romans 1:20. In other words, we are able to look around at nature, the cosmos, and even ourselves to recognize that this is the work of an intelligent and intentional Designer. He has pre-programmed us with this basic understanding and to suppress this truth is wickedness.

Next, we come into agreement, or *covenant,* with Him. This would have been covered in the repentance step that you should have already taken, if you are reading this. Repentance positions us to receive the Holy Spirit, beginning the sanctification process that allows our relationship with the Father to flourish. This is where things get tricky. Today's faith leaders have not done a respectable job of explaining that the basis of this relationship is not negotiable. It's not a democracy. I am not implying that Yah doesn't take our thoughts, desires, and feelings into consideration, particularly those that we have been courageous enough to express. The Most High

---

[103] Hebrews 11:6

does not want robots as children. What I am referring to is the very foundation of our relationship with Him. We have been subtly taught that we can have a relationship with the Most High on our own terms rather than the ones that He has set forth in Scripture.

The Father, the Son, and all of their prophets have the same message: repent from your sins and place your trust in Elohiym. It does not say *"believe in Jesus and obedience is optional."* There is no separation between the two. The Messiah says that if you love Me, you will obey my commandments. He and the Father are one. The commandments are the same.

Furthermore, obedience does not end with repentance from sin. One who simply labors to abstain from sin without any further effort is involved in empty religion. Spiritual disciplines, such as prayer and Bible study, are only optional if you are not part of the Kingdom of the Most High.

Those who proclaim the Messiah as Savior are commanded to obey the house rules set by the Father and follow the example of the Son. To ignore these things is an indication that we have created our own god and are in functional idolatry.

Principle 2: Get to Know Him

Truly getting to know someone has become a lost art. In many cases, we have a relationship with an idea of a person rather than the actual individual in front of us. This is the result of entering into relationships with the primary focus on getting our needs met. We are often more concerned about how a person makes us feel, what they can contribute to our lives, and how they make us look. This hinders us from going beyond the surface level of getting to know them apart from the role they play in our lives. While it's good to be aware of what characteristics we are looking for in a partner, it can be easy to lose sight of the person as independent from us, rather than a mere extension.

There is an even greater temptation for this to occur in our relationship with the Most High because well, we do need Him for everything. The relationship is also prone to becoming one sided since we cannot tangibly engage Him in the way that we are used to with humans. For instance, if we have not been taught both how to listen for the voice of Yah and the importance of waiting on Him, our prayer life may consist of us doing 99.9% of the talking.

If we desire a close intimate relationship with our Elohiym, we must experience Him holistically. Everyone desires to be known. No wife wants her spouse's interest in her to be limited to her cooking, cleaning, and child rearing abilities. No husband wants to only be acknowledged when it's time to pay the bills, fix problems, or protect against threats. We have all been wonderfully made in Yah's image: layered, complex, and multi-dimensional just like our Father. Keep in mind that while He is not human, He is a person with feelings. Just as we have an innate desire to be deeply known and share ourselves, so does He.

Communication is the most effective tool in getting to know someone, with observation being a close-second. On a basic level, we understand that effective communication on the part of the speaker entails clear and authentic articulation. A thoughtful response, nourished by active listening, is the responsibility of the receiver. What is often forgotten is the element of curiosity. Sometimes we do not truly know the people we are connected to because we're not curious enough to ask. This includes asking questions that convey genuine interest in, not only the subject at hand, but also in the other person's perspective on the matter. If relationship building is the goal, whether we agree or disagree, at the very least we should care enough to know how our loved ones arrive at their conclusions. Aside from asking a person direct questions about themselves, this is another powerful way to get to know someone.

It bears repeating that we are often so focused on how the other person can meet our needs or fit into our lives that we lose sight of the fact that he or she is an autonomous person. A healthy individual will have thoughts, interests, and desires that are separate from us or our relationship. Ideally, they would be aligned or at-least complimentary; either way it's important to see people apart from ourselves.

This same principle can be applied to our relationship with the Most High. He undoubtedly existed before our creation and had an entire Heavenly Kingdom even before the earth was formed. Although we are made in His image and very precious to Him, He does have desires that go beyond making sure we have a decent job, spouse, and impeccable health. As the Creator of all things, it would make sense that He would have an opinion on everything. We should keep in mind that the Scriptures are meant to be a guide, but they do not capture every single thought and desire of the Most High. Although His written Word is a treasure to us, we are meant to have a relationship with Yahuah that transcends book, chapter, and verse. I know that is scary for some to consider but we can take comfort that the Father will never contradict His Word nor His character as revealed in Scripture.

We would be surprised at what we could find if we took our eyes off ourselves long enough to inquire of the Most High regarding things that don't necessarily concern us, but allow us to grow in our understanding of Him. Some examples of this would be:

- Asking Him why certain things were created and their intended function.

- Asking what He meant by a specific Scripture or why He commanded certain things.

- Asking for His perspective on current events.

- Asking for insight/revelation on both Biblical and non-biblical historical events.

The more first-hand information we collect, the more intimate our relationship with Him will become. Keep in mind that this is a process and there are things that He will develop within us during this time such as humility and patience. He may not respond immediately, or He may answer in a way that we did not expect, revealing His many vessels of communication. There may also be times where He is not interested in speaking about the topic that we are currently broaching. I have had instances when I've approached Him about a specific matter, and He abruptly changes the subject. I'm left thinking, "Okay, well, moving on!" While I find it hilarious, I also acknowledge that whatever He's choosing to convey at that moment is what is most important. So, I happily table my topic and get on board with His program. Just know that any time spent engaging the Most High is never a waste. In fact, as we walk with Him, we will see that He does not waste anything. He has a fascinating way of bringing things full circle, even things our human minds have long forgotten.

In short, we want to know our Elohiym for ourselves. Many of us grew up with an understanding of Yah through the perspective of our parents, grandparents, and church family. Today's generation is inundated with faith-based "influencers" from which we get our ideas about the Most High and what our relationship should look like. The danger in this is that we all see Him through a lens. The Scripture alludes to this when it says we see through a dimly lit glass.[104] This lens includes religious conditioning, trauma, our personal experiences and personalities. Imagine trying to get to know Him through someone else's lens. Of course, we can be encouraged by fellow Believers, but it is the will of the Father for us to get to know Him ourselves based on the framework revealed in nature and in His Word.

Principle 3: Reciprocity

If acknowledgment and agreement serve as the foundation, and communication is the building block(s), then reciprocity is the element that validates the relationship. I am certain that those of us who have encountered one-sided friendships or romantic partnerships eventually came to the sober realization that they were not, in fact, relationships at all. We were simply being used for whatever the other party stood to gain from us. Throughout Scripture, we see Yahuah pleading with His bride, Israel, to return His loyalty and affection. At one point He demonstrated His pain and frustration through the life of His prophet Hosea who was commanded to marry an unfaithful harlot.[105] Anyone who has experienced unrequited love can empathize with our Creator.

Unlike humans, our relationship with the Most High is solely based on His desire for us, rather than need. Psalm 50:12 says, ***"If I were hungry, I would not tell you, for the world is mine, and all that is in it."*** The Scriptures say that if we do not praise Him the rocks will cry out in our place.[106] In Isaiah 40:13-14 He asks, "***Who***

---

[104] 1 Corinthians 13:12

[105] Hosea 1:2

[106] Luke 19:37-40

has measured the Spirit of Adonai? Who has been His counselor, instructing Him? Whom did He consult, to gain understanding? Who taught Him how to judge, taught Him what He needed to know, showed Him how to discern?"

In short there is no physical, emotional, or mental need that we can fulfill in the Father. We are even replaceable when it comes to the work of the Kingdom. The Most High has created us uniquely for certain purposes but should we forfeit our mantles, Yah will find someone else who is willing to serve Him wholeheartedly. Our minds must be renewed to the understanding that it is an honor to be loved by the King of Kings and a privilege to give back to the One who has given so much.

These humbling words should bring beauty to the fact that despite us having so little to offer, He still yearns to be close to us. Everyone likes to feel needed, but there is something special about being *chosen.* The Creator chose us because we are His children, made in His image. Babies come into the world as bona-fide takers, offering nothing except being our look-a-likes, an occasional lop-sided smile, and that fresh newborn smell. Yet, over time, even children are expected to begin reciprocating. For many of us, we would be hard pressed to repay our parents for the sacrifices they have made. Thankfully, they delight in our efforts of appreciation.

How do we reciprocate the love of the Father whose love supersedes anything that we will ever experience elsewhere? What can you give someone who owns everything? When we consider all that He is and all that He has given us, the only reasonable answer would be our whole being. Remember that our relationship with Him is frequently depicted in Scripture using marital terminology. Years ago, someone said to me that the goal of marriage is to out love one another so that there is no lack. Realistically, we could never "out love" the Most High, but we can still have a beautiful time trying. When we think about how much He has given of Himself to us, our entire being, our lives, is really the only acceptable offering.

Ideally, this sounds good but what does that look like on a practical level? Essentially, it is the working out of Him being on the thrones of our hearts. It is our loyalty to Him and our hatred of idolatry. It is time invested diligently seeking Him both through Scripture and personally. It's offering up spontaneous moments of praise, worship, and thanksgiving just because. It's consistent communication which includes speaking *and* listening. It is considering what He would think before we speak and do. It is obedience to His laws, statutes, and commandments. It's bragging about Him and sharing His goodness that others may be reconciled with Him. It's intentionally dying to ourselves that He may live inside us and His glory be made manifest to the world. What else would be a proper response to an Elohiym who has everything but still desires *intimacy* with us? While we can never repay Yah for all that He has done, we must be honest with ourselves in how we are reciprocating His love.

Principle 4: Love & Commitment

By now, we have all heard that love is an action word. Simply believing in Yahusha does not guarantee salvation. Remember the demons knew who He was, too. [107] Our understanding transcends head knowledge when our actions begin to align with what we believe. The Scriptures tell us to *work out* our salvation meaning that our faith is proven by our works. [108] John 14:15 has already been

---

[107] Acts 19:15

[108] Philippians 2:12

quoted several times in this writing as we are reminded that Yahusha sees obedience to His commandments as a demonstration of our love for Him.

When we commit to the Most High, it is not for a season. It is not just for the good times. It is a covenant, in the likeness of marriage, which requires faithfulness for better or for worse. This means when we fall ill, experience loss or misfortune, we remain committed even if doing so through tears of pain and frustration. Our commitment will be tested and proven by our ability to endure our respective races to the end.

During the time of the disciples, they considered those that turned away from the faith as never really being with them in the first place.[109] While there are a lot of opinions on the topic of salvation, I side with our Hebrew ancestors. I find it difficult to understand how someone could behold the King of glory, through the process of being born again and turn away. What would we be turning to when we have the knowledge that earthly joys and pains are temporal, and our hope lies in eternal promises? While they may not have been privy to all the convoluted theological doctrines of today, this simple understanding is what brought many of our people through the harsh realities of chattel slavery.

Commitment is not just about enduring to the end. It is also about how we endure, which brings us back to love. There are marriages that have lasted for 30, 40, or even 50 years, yet they are functionally dead. The love and tenderness that once filled the relationship have faded, leaving only a sense of duty to bind the couple together. This reminds me of the message given to the assembly of Ephesus.[109] Here Yahusha, who is the head of the

---

[109] Revelations 2:1-4

called-out assembly, commonly referred to as the church, commends them for their hard work, patience, and intolerance for evil and false teachers. Despite all of that, He says that they do not love Him or one another as they first did! He also goes on to say that if they do not repent from this and turn back to Him to do the things they did when they first believed, then He would remove their lamp stand from its place among the assemblies.

This shows us that this is not something to be taken lightly. In short, Yah is saying do not come half stepping when it comes to our relationship with Him. It is not enough to just go through the motions to fulfill our religious duties and prevent eternal damnation. In fact, this is reminiscent of a pharisaical spirit. Sure, the Pharisees obeyed the laws, statutes, and commandments, but they lacked true love for their Elohiym and one another. Yah rightfully expects our passion for Him to burn feverishly and continuously.

CHAPTER 13

Time & Worship

After reviewing some foundational principles for a successful relationship, it's time to discuss how to make intimacy with the Most High a reality. While we should work to identify and actively remove hindrances, it should not delay us in taking strides to deepen our connection to Him. This is an ongoing process but the purer we are in spirit, the more access we will be granted to our Creator.

Time & Intimacy

A key factor in increasing intimacy is the element of time. We wouldn't expect to build a fruitful marriage by only spending 5-10 minutes per day with our spouse. I'm not going to quantify how much time we should be investing, but again, it would be helpful to compare what we are doing with our time to how much of it we're spending in the presence of the Most High. In a day, we might spend an hour at the gym, watch a one-hour television show, scroll through social media for another hour, and then spend another hour texting or talking with friends. Yet, we managed to let a mere 10-minute devotional be the highlight of our quality time with Yah? As the saying goes, we make time for what we want to make time for. Nevertheless, we all start from somewhere and as we grow, our desire for more of Him should increase.

A renewal of the mind is a necessity because we need Yah's help to properly align our priorities to understand what truly matters and what does not. An eternal perspective can increase our awareness of what is temporary versus what is everlasting that we may build our treasures for the latter.[110] Personally, spending adequate time with Yah has been the singularly best investment of my life. My relationship with the Most High showed me how much I did not know, and it's not limited to spiritual things, although everything is connected in some aspect.

When we repent and accept Messiah, there is a veil that is removed from our eyes, and we begin to see things differently. It is a progressive journey of layers being peeled back, allowing for greater knowledge, and understanding of the Creator, ourselves, and the world around us. It is a very humbling process because, as more is revealed, we realize just how much Yah has kept us, even in our ignorance. Here, the depths of His grace become clear, leading us to that broken and contrite heart spoken of in Psalm 51:17. It is a sign of understanding, humility, and gratefulness.

All of this takes time. Recalling the different lenses that we see through, these same layers must be broken down: religious programming, fear of man, trauma, and how we view the world based upon our individual make-up and experiences. The type of deep soul work that the Holy Spirit must complete will not take place with a 5–10-minute daily devotional. I don't have anything against devotionals, but they should be used in addition to our daily reading of the Word, not in place of. Through His prophets, the Creator gifted us a book about Himself. Why would we then go and entirely replace divine revelation with a think piece written by humans?

A fascinating characteristic of the Most High is that we cannot out give Him. This means when we give Him more of our time, He supernaturally makes sure we have time for the other things that we

---

[110] Matthew 6:19-21

need, emphasis on the word *need* not *want* as wisdom is required in all things. Once we adopt the mindset that the presence of Yah is precious and demands a sacrifice of time, our next question becomes: how do we allocate that time? Well, if we have breath in our bodies then we should never be short on praise. This leads us to our first spiritual discipline, praise and worship.

Praise and Worship

Praise and worship ushers in the Spirit of the Most High. It's how we get His attention only to then shower Him with ours. Praise is an expression of honor for Yah, acknowledging who He is and all that He has done. Worship refers to the posture of obedience and submission behind our words and actions.

Praise and worship doesn't have to be confined to putting on music and singing along. We can freestyle with lyrics and melodies from our hearts, specific to how we see and experience the Father for ourselves. If you know how to play an instrument, all the better. Instead of speaking in tongues, you may also sing in your heavenly language. Dancing can be incorporated into our time of praise and worship as well. Simply learn to be sensitive to the Spirit and move how He is leading you. It may feel silly at first but remember that you are in the secret place of the Most High where you are safe to be your authentic self. Whether you can sing or have rhythm is completely irrelevant. This is when it is proper to lean on the phrase, *"Yah knows my heart!"* To the brothers, don't be afraid to express yourselves as well. Remember King David, a mighty man of war, worshipped through song, dance, instruments, and poetry. He publicly shared his worship without a care for who was watching, so surely you can be vulnerable when you're alone with your Heavenly Father.

It's important to note that praise and worship is not optional. I recall hearing people say they would skip the praise and worship part of church services because they just came to hear the Word. I perceived this to mean that they were only there to receive with no intention of giving. This goes back to what we discussed about reciprocity. It also speaks to the idea that people disregard the feelings of our Heavenly Father. We also seem to forget that He is a King. The King of Kings to be exact. Why would we think it is okay to enter His presence without an offering? Adding insult to injury is the fact that what He is currently requiring of us, is free. It costs nothing to sing His praises and to lift our hands in worship. However, this has not always been the case.

When Yah was teaching the ancient Israelites how to worship Him, they were required to bring forth various types of sacrificial offerings. The book of Leviticus delves into this matter in great detail. Not only were sacrificial offerings mandatory, but there are numerous divinely inspired Scriptures that instruct us to praise Him through singing, dancing, and musical instruments.[111] Even Cain and Abel had to bring forth a physical offering. Never in history has it been appropriate for us to show up to the foot of His throne empty handed. Not only is He worthy but hearing us singing His praises blesses the Father and He delights in it. Are you aware that the Scripture says that He sings over us as well? Zephaniah 3:17 tells us ***"Yahuah Elohayka in the midst of you is mighty, He will save, He will rejoice over you with joy, He will rest in his love, he will joy over you with singing."***

These were words spoken to Israel as a result of their repentance. So as repentant Believers who are now enjoying an intimate

---

[111] Psalm 149:3

relationship with the Most High, we can expect for Yah to have the same disposition towards us. What a beautiful and loving Elohiym we serve!

Praise and worship are necessary parts of our quality time with the Most High. It has the power to transform our time, our relationship with Him, and even our lives. There are Believers who spend most of their time with Yah in worship. From there, He begins to respond to them and lead them in prayer; so, do not skip out on this. We may not always have time for a full out song and dance session but simple offerings of thanksgiving on the way to work are always appropriate. Overall, be sure that in the time you are setting aside for the Father, you are putting your all into giving Him the adoration that He deserves.

CHAPTER 14

Prayers of Refinement

Talking is the primary way in which we engage our fellow human beings. Prayer is used exclusively to describe communication with our Creator. While we know that prayer is essential, it is crucial to consider *what* we pray. In Chapter 12 we pushed the parameters of prayer to include asking Yah about Himself and about the world that He created. In this chapter we want to focus on prayers of refinement.

Refinement is defined by the improvement or clarification of something by the making of minor changes. When we send up prayers of refinement, we have already put away the sins of the flesh. At this juncture, we may even be tempted to believe in our own goodness. We know that we're not intentionally taking part in sin and when ungodly thoughts or attitudes surface, we are quick to shut them down and repent. Yet this is when we need the eyes of the Holy One who sees everything. We all have blind spots and many of us are too defensive to have another human being point them out to us. As a culture, we also struggle with "pointing things out" in love demonstrated by the three t's: tact, tone, and timing.

Purity of Heart

There are several examples in Scripture of our ancestors asking Yah to search them. Not only do we need to be searched, but we also need a full heart transplant. Jeremiah 17:9-10 says ***"The heart is deceitful above all things, and desperately wicked: who can know it? I Yahuah search the heart, I try the mind, even to give every*** *man according to his ways, and according to the fruit of his doings."* Regardless of our self-perception, we would be wise to proactively ask the Most High to search us. This provides us with the opportunity to rectify any lingering wrongs concealed beneath the surface. I often request to be searched and to have anything that is not of Him removed. I also ask Yah to bring anything that I may have missed to my attention if it is something I need to actively repent of.

After requesting to be searched, we need to ask Yah to grant us pureness of heart along with a right spirit. Although the beauty of this world is quickly fading, it may still be hard to fully recognize how entrenched in sin we're in. When I say "we" I'm not necessarily talking about us as individuals, but rather the world as a whole. I'm referring to how the world is run as a system, the *Beast* system to be exact. Those with spiritual sight can perceive that the world, and how it is run, is in direct opposition to the Most High. It is worsening by the day and truthfully the pull of sin is too strong for us to be delivered on our own. This is why the heavy lifting is the work of the Holy Spirit. Our responsibility is to be willing and there are even times when we must ask for help with that. The Messiah said it best in Matthew 26:41 *"...the spirit is indeed willing but the flesh is weak."* And so, a refining prayer similar to the ones below, is something that should be recited regularly:

"Create a clean heart in me, O Elohiym, and renew a faithful spirit within me. Do not force me away from your presence, and do not take Ruach Qodesh from me. Restore the joy of your salvation to me, and provide me with a spirit of willing obedience."—Psalm 51:10-12

<u>Renewing of the Mind</u>

Another prayer of refinement that we will discuss involves the renewing of our minds. In my own walk, I have noticed there are times that I am unable to see how off I am in an area until the Holy Spirit has done some refining transformation. It is in retrospect that I can see where I once was. Bear in mind that we are all operating in a measure of spiritual blindness. This is why it's important that all Believers, but particularly those that are single and do not have children to have some measure of community. The Most High uses others as a mirror to reveal aspects of ourselves that need refining. Often, we won't know that we changed until Yah allows a situation to occur and we realize that we've responded differently than we had in the past. Our response should be to glorify the Father, giving thanks for the work He has done in us!

Renewing of the mind will rid us of the worldly residue that remains as a result of still being in the world, though not of the world.[112] It will take us off the broad road of what seems right and instead inspire us to consult the Most High on all things. This may seem excessive until we realize that the god of this world has perverted everything and we need Yah's wisdom for protection and prosperity.

After my born-again experience in 2017, I was walking in repentance of the sins of the flesh. I was in love with the Most High and active in my church. At that time, had someone referred to me as *worldly,* I would have been sorely offended. However, looking back, they would have had a point. While the Most High had already made significant changes in me, it wasn't until years later when I met my prayer partner that I realized how worldly I was. This

---

[112] John 17:15-16

person never made mention of it and honestly, she may not have even realized it, as it has nothing to do with sin. Yah brought us together supernaturally and we quickly bonded over our love for Him and our desire to live lives that are pleasing to Him.

There were undoubtedly a lot of things that I learned from her when it came to caring for my body. We have adopted some unnatural ways of doing things because of the convenience they provide. Because they have been so widely accepted, it hadn't dawned on me how toxic they were. This led me to making significant changes in the soaps I use to cleanse my body, beauty care, and even feminine hygiene products. It may be hard to connect the dots on what this has to do with creating intimacy with the Father. This is because in the Western world, we generally don't understand how the conditions of our physical bodies affect our spirit man. We will talk more about this later in the chapter on fasting.

In the same vein, I've recently overheard my prayer partner in conversation about not eating fruits without seeds in it. Why? Because shouldn't all fruit bear seed? Sure, it may be inconvenient to eat around the seeds but how does eating genetically modified food affect our bodies? Even when it comes to our healthcare, the Most High has given us everything that we need to care and heal ourselves. Yet some of us will not even pray before seeking medical advice from man. Anything the doctor prescribes, or the FDA approves, we willingly consume. This is an aspect of worldliness that we often do not think about. For the record, I'm not advising anyone to forgo seeking medical attention. I am suggesting that we seek guidance from the Most High first and have Him order our steps. This is a way of acknowledging Him in all our ways. We should be willing to profess Him as the Creator of our bodies and the One who owns the knowledge and power to bring healing. These are some of the benefits that we enjoy when we have an intimate relationship with the Father.

Since being born again, I have made a habit of praying for the renewing of my mind. As a result, Yah had already dealt with me on many topics such as how I viewed politics, eating clean according to Scripture, pagan holidays, etc. Yet through the influence of my prayer partner, my ability to apply Scripture to my life was elevated. This taught me to focus on Biblical prophecy rather than politics yet still be able to discern how the two were connected. My eating habits became even more refined, and I began to learn how to observe Biblical Holy Days and Feast Days. I have included this bit to show how Yah answered my prayers for a renewed mind. There are things that He taught me directly and later used another individual to help *refine* those areas. We should not compare ourselves to one another as Yahusha Ha'Mashiach is still our greatest example of righteousness. However, sometimes others may serve as a reference point of where we are in our spiritual walk.

Overall, a renewed mind is part of the perfecting process of being set-apart. This means that there are many things that we must unlearn and relearn. It requires a level of humility to accept that just because we've been seeing and doing things a certain way for years, or even decades, doesn't make it right. A renewed mind will also affect how we view the Father. It will deliver us from putting Him in a box, placed there by religion or even our own minds. It will cause us to see things from His perspective and prioritize His Kingdom. Above all, it is having the mind of Mashiach[113] who came not to do His own will but that of the Father.

---

[113] 1 Corinthians 2:16

We can craft prayers about the renewing of the mind based on Romans 12:2 which reads: ***"And be not conformed to this world: but be ye transformed by the renewal of your mind, that ye may prove what is that good, and acceptable, and perfect will of Elohiym."***

A Final Word on Refining Prayer

This chapter is meant to help us go beyond prayers of simply getting our needs met. Matthew 6:25-34 goes into detail about how the Father already knows about our basic needs. This does not mean that we should not bring a dire need before Him. Our faith is strengthened when we take a need to the Father and see Him deliver. My hope is that we don't get stuck there. A pure heart and renewed mind will enable your spirit man to help you endure seasons where Yah may allow your physical needs to lack. We should also be praying regularly for others as every Believer is called to be an intercessor for our fellow brothers and sisters as well as those who are lost.

This is why I insist that our relationship with the Most High is a serious investment of time. We are praying to get to know Him, to discern His will for our lives, to be delivered, refined, for our own needs, and for the needs of others. There are times when we are simply speaking to Him as a friend, telling Him what's on our minds, how we feel about things, and sometimes just delighting in Him with laughter as we share inside jokes. This is easily prayer alone! This does not include praise and worship, reading Scripture, meditation, etc.

It may seem overwhelming but be encouraged that when we ask to be changed, Yahuah will absolutely deliver on that. There are certain prayers that I can pray with such boldness because I know that I am praying according to His will, which is for us to be transformed into His image in the likeness of the Holy One, Yahusha Ha'Mashiach. When we walk in repentance, the refining process is often subtle and less painful compared to the initial, significant leap we took in deciding to die to ourselves and live for our Creator.

I'm not implying that our walk with the Most High is always easy as it still requires a daily dying to the flesh. The difference is, it is something that you actually want to do, being empowered to do so by the Holy Spirit. This is what the Scripture means by the power of sin being *broken* in our lives as we are no longer slaves to it. We are now free to serve our Elohiym in righteousness and able to discern the rewards that prayers of refinement bring, the greatest of those being an increase in intimacy with the Most High.

CHAPTER 15

Listening Prayer

Growing up Baptist, the prevailing thought was that Yah primarily spoke to us through His Word. My use of the word *primarily* is generous as I have rarely heard of any other way acknowledged outside of an occasional nod to the Holy Spirit for bringing a thought to mind. Throughout my spiritual journey, there were times where I felt as if Yah was ordering my steps, but I was never specifically taught how to listen for His voice. Thankfully, my last church home had a heart for Believers to hear from the Father for themselves. There, I learned to quiet myself in order to hear from the Holy Spirit. This was done in-house as well as through a para ministry that brought Believers from all over Los Angeles together to grow in discerning His voice and encourage one another.

Early in that ministry, I had a life changing experience. A few weeks prior to one of the meet ups, I had been privately lamenting about some things to the Most High in my journal. As a scribe of sorts, I love using an analogy to describe how I'm feeling. So, I wrote to Yah explaining how, "I feel like I'm in a long corridor full of doors with windows. Outside the windows I can see people doing all the things that I want to do but every time I try to open the door to partake, I find that it's locked. There are some doors that even appear open, but as soon as I get close, they slam shut and lock on me." I never told a soul about how I was feeling nor about the journal entry.

Fast forward about three weeks later to one of my first city-wide listening prayer sessions. There was a younger brother there named

Pernel that I had never met. He asked Jesus how he could pray for and or encourage me. After a few moments of silence He said, "God showed me you in a long hallway full of locked doors and He said He's going to give you the key to every single one of those doors." I don't know what I was expecting but it certainly was not for a stranger to read aloud what I had written in secret to my Elohiym a few weeks ago. The Holy Spirit also gave him a Bible verse for me which Yah has used to confirm things for me ever since.

Up until that point, the prophetic, to my knowledge, had never been a part of my spiritual journey. Yet, I came for a word, had the faith to receive, and receive I did. That ministry proved to be an ongoing blessing as the words from other Spirit filled Believers continue to manifest in my life even to this day. In this chapter, I'll be sharing some of what I learned from that time as well as some things I have been taught by the Holy Spirit since being called out of the church.

Belief & Discernment

To begin the journey of hearing the voice of the Most High, we must first believe that He speaks. That belief alone will need to surpass our doubts, ignorance, and even religious dogma that puts Him in a box. This also correlates to how we see Him. Do we view Yahuah as a harsh and demanding Elohiym that is waiting to punish us for the slightest infraction? Is our idea of Him a cold, distant Creator who has set things in motion but has little intervention in human affairs? Perhaps we've subconsciously concluded that while Yah was involved during Biblical times, He has a more hands off approach today. Sometimes we must pause to ask ourselves if what we have been taught, or even the assumptions that we've come to on our own, make sense?

Even the book of Revelation takes a break from the impending doom and gloom to inform us that Yah created everything for His pleasure[114] and that includes us. Did He not create the first two people and fellowship with them in the cool of the day? Didn't He personally intervene in the lives of our Israelite ancestors as a nation and with individuals? Does He not tell us that He is a rewarder of those who diligently seek Him? What are we seeking Him for? Is it so that He can feel wanted but never offer any kind of response?

If you are a Believer, you should know that you were created for a purpose. You may still be struggling with the specifics of it but the Most High created you to complete an assignment(s) on the earth. It is His preference that you answer that call rather than Him needing to get a substitute. Surely, the purpose will be fulfilled whether we play our role or not. By not being intentional, we deprive ourselves of reaching our full potential and the eternal reward that awaits us. We also deny the Most High the glory of witnessing His creation functioning as He intended.

Therefore, if Yah alone knows the full scope of our destinies, and it is obvious that as a fallen people we will need His help to fulfill it, then would it not make sense for Him to communicate with us? Furthermore, we are in the 21st century. How can the Bible alone always speak to the particulars of our situation today? Yes, there are principles for every matter because there is nothing new under the sun. However, sometimes we need more than that. We were designed for more than that. We were created for relationship with our Creator. Let's get it in our heads that Yah wants to speak to us and that He indeed does.

---

[114] Revelation 4:11

Nevertheless, it can be difficult for the carnal mind to wrap its head around what the voice of the Most High sounds like. With brains solely fluent in human communication, the learning curve can be steep. One of the main things I learned in listening prayer are the ways in which Yah can choose to speak. The various "channels" include Scripture, people, nature, media, dreams, visions, our own thoughts and more. I also know that many of us were taught that numbers were the boogeyman, but this is a result of Western religious programming. Numbers have meaning and even the Hebrew alphabet has corresponding numerical value, referred to as the gematria.

Although the Scriptures were not originally numbered, the Most High at times supernaturally works through that as well. For example, I had been seeing 11:11 for a very long time. Later, I learned that verses marked as 11:11 often denote a transition into a promise which can be either positive, as in Isaiah 11:11, or negative, as in Jeremiah 11:11. As my understanding increased, I was led to different books of the Bible that contained this chapter and verse combination and it served as a confirmation of what Yah had already been speaking to me about. Of course, not every single verse with 11:11 will line up with this exact principle. This is why it is important to have a relationship with the Holy Spirit so that you understand who you are, what season you're in, and be able to discern what applies to you.

The Sovereign One has the ability to communicate with His creation through any means He chooses. It is up to us to believe, quiet ourselves as we seek Him, wait patiently with expectation, and grow in discerning His voice. Next, we're going to discuss three practices that can put us on the road to doing just that.

Biblical Understanding

Knowing Scripture is crucial to hearing from the Most High. It is how we *fact check* as the voice of Yah will never contradict His Word nor His principles. We will not know that if we don't know His Word or His nature. As explained before, the Bible is not solely a rule book, but it also gives us insight into the personality of the Creator. His Word tells us what He finds pleasure in as well as what He finds abominable.

For instance, Yah tells us not to commit adultery. Therefore, we can be sure that if we hear a voice encouraging us to pursue a married person, then that is not Him. We do not have to look for a sign or seek confirmation because at the root of the matter, Yah has already given an answer as it violates His law and His nature, which is faithfulness. This doesn't mean that we must have the entire Bible read and memorized before Yah can speak to us. However, the Word says that the Holy Spirit will bring all things to our remembrance.[115] It has to already be in us for it to be recalled. When we do not know the Word or have a firm grasp of Yahuah's character based on Scripture, that means we will have to put greater effort into ensuring that what we are hearing is from Yah.

Thankfully in the age of Google, we are easily able to find corresponding Scriptures for a variety of topics. Yet, it's not always as simple as a touch of a button since the Word must be read in context. This requires maturity and integrity because it is easy to take isolated texts as confirmation of what it is that we desire. We will go more in depth on this topic later in the chapter on the principles of Bible study.

---

[115] John 14:26

<u>Dying to Self</u>

Prior to 2020, I had multiple opportunities to move to Texas. The headquarters for the company I had been employed at for several years was in Houston. My manager along with other members of corporate staff would gently encourage me to make the move. At the time, I was dating a guy that made mention of us moving to Austin. Both were a hard "no" for me. Outside of Florida, I was never really drawn to the South. As for Texas, the sweltering heat sans a nearby ocean to cool off in was a dealbreaker. There was also the unbelievable size and quantity of bugs that the state seemed to produce. (Spoiler alert: I've gotten bit by mosquitos more times in one day than the 12 years I lived in California.) I would gladly deal with high rent and traffic for the comfort of pleasant weather, beach access, and fewer bugs. Not to mention, I just really loved L.A. and the life I had created there over the years. I barely knew anyone in Texas, and I certainly was not planning to move anywhere with someone I wasn't married to.

Amid lockdowns during the summer of 2020, I made the decision to leave my church and solely focus on my relationship with the Most High. Although I knew that my time was up at my current church, I assumed that once the Covid thing blew over, Yah would eventually lead me to another community. Meanwhile I entered an intense season of praise, worship, fasting, and journaling.

By August, I had begun following an on-line ministry in which the leader called for an 8 day corporate fast. During this time the Most High's voice was clearer than ever. Among a host of other revelations given during that period were explicit instructions to relocate to Texas. I knew immediately that this was Yah's voice because no way in a million years would I have even considered making this move. Left to my own devices, I may have lived happily ever after in my L.A. studio indefinitely. Nevertheless, I was on such a spiritual high, from hearing so clearly from my Heavenly Father that there was little room for disappointment. At the time, I also believed the move to be temporary. I was sure that I would be coming back to L.A. in about a year or so. Four years, 3 insufferable summers, and dozens of mosquito bites later, I'm still here. I digress.

Jokes aside, while this may not be my preferred place of residence, I am still blessed more than I could have imagined because of my obedience in relocating. Spiritually, I grew beyond what I thought was possible. When I experienced that breakthrough during the fast in August of 2020, I felt like I had reached the pinnacle of my spiritual journey. However, I had no idea that I was just getting started. That is the fascinating aspect about being in Mashiach, there are always new levels to ascend to, including those that we were not fully aware existed.

I'm sharing this testimony to demonstrate the importance of dying to our own desires. It is an absolute game changer and the more we die to our own will, the more confident we will become in discerning the voice of the Most High. For clarity, dying to our own desires does not mean we become an avatar of ourselves that no longer has wants or preferences. Yet, the will of the Most High must trump everything else. Our desires must be placed on the back-burner and only allowed to come into fruition if and when the will of the Most High calls it forth.

We can also take comfort in the fact that He places desires within us. Oftentimes our character is not prepared to receive what we are asking for. So, although it may be counter intuitive, as a Believer it is the wise thing to do. The Most High might even purify our desires by transforming our motivations for the things that we want. He could also deliver us in a way that the thing that we desire is no longer an idol. Basically, we will be in a healthier place, spiritually, to receive what we are asking for. The point being that the desire itself is usually not the problem but rather a matter of timing and the need for us to go through a period of preparation beforehand.

"For whoever desires to save his life will lose it, but whoever loses his life for My sake will find it." —Matthew 16:25

This verse is not only referring to our lives in a physical sense. Yes, we should be willing to give our lives if that is what's required of us for the sake of our Messiah. But "life" also refers to the hopes, dreams, and goals that we envision for ourselves. This must all be handed over in faith that what the Most High gives back to us will be better than anything we could have ever dreamt up on our own. When it comes to listening prayer, dying to self is important because it eliminates at least one voice from the chatter in our minds, reducing confusion. We may still face the voice of the enemy, who seeks to instill fear and doubt. Additionally, we might encounter loved ones who struggle to understand the direction Yah is leading us. Nevertheless, let Yah be true and everyone else be a liar. Trust in His plan and move forward with His leading.

Seeking & Perceiving

It is not always the will of the Most High to miraculously fix our situations at once. Sometimes He allows us to go through a process to get to the other side. If we surrender to it, our character will be refined, and we will experience a deeper connection with our Father. I'm admittedly a fan of the soft life to the extent that the Most High will allow. Therefore, I shamelessly ask Him to fix things, supernaturally. Yet, it is always contingent upon His will. If He wants me to go through a process, then so be it as I wholeheartedly trust that He knows what is best for me.

Having said that, when a process is necessary, a part of it involves seeking Him for answers on how to navigate the situation. According to Matthew 7:7-8, if we are seeking then we should be expecting to find. This is where listening prayer comes in. Since we're no longer simply venting about our grievances, needs, and desires, but rather asking questions about how to maneuver the circumstances, we should now be actively listening for answers and/or instructions.

I believe that the Most High speaks to us a lot more than we think. A measure of pride deceives us into assuming ourselves more independent than we are. In my own walk, I've discovered that I am more needy than I once thought. A life of faith that removes you from dependency on jobs, people, or systems will quickly bring this to light. Psalms 103:14 reads ***"As a father has compassion on his children, so the LORD has compassion <u>on those who fear him;</u> For He knows our frame; He remembers that we are dust."***

I often wonder how many times angels have been working overtime on my behalf while I was absentmindedly driving, cooking, swimming in the ocean, and so on. I don't think we truly grasp just how vulnerable we are. However, our Father says that He does and is compassionate toward us. And what do compassionate Fathers do? They warn, lead, guide, and counsel. Understanding this should tell us that Yahuah is constantly communicating with us in some form or fashion. The issues are:

a) Do we fear Him?

b) Do we perceive Him?

If we do not fear Him and function as if we don't need Him, then we should not expect the compassion that the verse above speaks of. For those of us who are intentionally seeking His will and to remain in the midst of it, help is available. The question remains; do we perceive it?

Per·ceive

(verb)

1. become aware or conscious of (something); come to realize or understand.

2. interpret or look on (someone or something) in a particular way; regard as.

Let's first recognize that the word *perceive* is a verb, indicating an action involved. Here are some helpful synonyms:

- Look on
- View
- Regard
- Consider
- Think of
- Judge
- Deem
- Appraise
- Assess
- Adjudge
- Figure out
- Size up
- Value
- Rate

- Suppose
- Think
- Sum up

From the definition and associated words, it's clear that the action here is mental. An important first step in perceiving is removing the idea of *coincidences* from our minds. Yes, there is such a thing, but for a Spirit filled Believer, it is more often the exception than the rule. Our lives will change when we begin to piece together that all these recurring messages from various sources are actually the Most High speaking to us.

Here I must caution for the need to be balanced. There is a temptation to go overboard where we allow everything to be a *confirmation* of some sort, but this always goes back to dying to self which helps us to remain sober in our perception. It also requires us to pray and meditate on what we believe we are being shown as we mature in our ability to perceive. In fact, praying, pondering, and at times fasting to properly discern what the Holy Spirit is saying to us will remain a constant in the life of a Believer.

As we grow, the complexity of the subject matter will increase. In the beginning we may need to pray and fast over carnal things because we are tuning our spirits to a new form of communication. An example of this may be a weighty decision about a job, moving, or family life. However, as we develop a closer relationship with Yah, and He begins to communicate mysteries to us, our level of perception will need to be heightened, requiring greater prayer, meditation, and fasting. There are levels to this.

Humility and expectation are other aspects of perceiving. Humility doesn't always seek grand gestures as it's often the small things in relationships that build intimacy; the things that only you and the other person know about. Private thoughts and inside jokes. Some of us are always so busy looking for big signs that we miss subtle messages from the Holy Spirit. We must be gracious and thankful for both the great and small as they all work together to point us in the right direction. We should also expect for our Creator to speak to us and be vigilant for His voice.

A Final Word on Perception

Belief, Biblical understanding, and dying to self are all easy concepts to understand, but perception can be ambiguous. In hopes of providing clarity through a real-life example I'm going to share the following testimony.

Recently, and unexpectedly, I started having digestive issues. I could have immediately prayed for healing while simultaneously making a doctor's appointment. In fact, that's how many of us function, sometimes without the prayer. Yet that is not seeking. Seeking was me first asking the Father if I even needed to go to the doctor. It may surprise some readers, but when the Most High reveals parts of the Beast System, which unfortunately includes the healthcare system, you'll find it to be a very relevant question. After all, they all collaborated to inject poison into our system in 2020 for the "greater good."

To my dismay, Yah answered this question with a yes. In fact, He used a cousin of mine to say verbatim, *twice,* that I needed a Primary Care Physician. She didn't even know what was going on with me. She was simply going off the fact that I had been visiting Urgent Care for upper respiratory issues. I heard Yah's voice through hers. So, I made an appointment with the doctor but regardless of what they said, I began seeking Yah to lead me to the right things for my body to begin the healing process. I looked up certain digestive organs online so that I could have a better understanding of what I was potentially dealing with. Underneath one of the articles was a video of a doctor describing my symptoms and recommending turmeric. *Coincidentally*, I had almost a full bottle in my medicine cabinet. I picked up what the Most High was putting down and immediately started a regime.

I was having a discussion with an older coworker who was also a Believer. We were discussing health in general and I mentioned the issue that I was facing. She immediately got on the phone with her friend who had knowledge of different teas used to treat various ailments. She put the lady on the phone, and I told her what was happening. She recommended that I take Dandelion tea, which I *coincidentally* had on hand as well. I incorporated that to the regimen, and then one day, I came across something on my social media feed about this IP6 powder that promotes immune health, so, I ordered some of that as well.

Shortly after, my lab results came back from the doctor's office. The physician's assistant let me know that my white blood cells were slightly low. She said it was nothing to be too concerned about, but she did take notice. Well, we know that white blood cells are involved in your immune system. Do you see the pattern yet? I was also experiencing bloating after meals. It *coincidentally* occurred to me that many Asian cultures consume hot tea after every meal to aid digestion. I added each of these things to my regime as they came and I began to experience significant relief in my systems.

This was a blessing because the procedure that the doctor scheduled me for to get a better look at what's going on was two months out. I mean, if it was something serious, would I even make it to 2 months? Madness. I am not keen on this procedure at all so I told the Most High He has two months to heal me and get me out of this thing. Perhaps by the time I've finished writing this book, I'll have an update on the situation which I will gladly report back.

I've shared this to illustrate what seeking the Most High and perceiving His response can look like in real time. Notice that all the other steps were included in this process as well. I applied Biblical understanding that informed me that Yah is both Creator and Healer. I believed that He can and is willing to heal me. I sought Him out on the matter and had a sense of expectation that He would answer me. I didn't dismiss the different ways the answer came to me,whether it was from someone else, the media, or even the Holy Spirit simply reminding me of something I already knew. I died to my own desire to NOT go to the doctor and instead followed His direction.

Listening prayer is one of the most effective tools for building intimacy with the Most High. Once we embark on the journey of hearing His voice, there's no turning back. We will experience a great measure of confidence and security. Most of all, you will know, without any doubt, that your Heavenly Father genuinely cares about everything concerning you.

CHAPTER 16

Prayer Journaling

In the era of venting on social media, sharing every new revelation, or constantly soliciting the opinions of others, beginning a habit of journaling can be transformational. There are times when we feel like we just have to say something, but it may not be our place or the right time to offer input. Perhaps we're not in the best emotional space to communicate effectively or we may be experiencing confusion on the matter. In situations like these, journaling can help relieve anxiety, organize our thoughts, and by proxy, improve our relationship with the Most High and others.

I got my first diary when I was around 9 years old. I still have it along with all of my subsequent ones. It was decades before I realized that the things that I wrote in my journal were not always my own thoughts. It's likely that most of the thoughts were mine prior to being born again. Looking back, I can see a progressive change in my subject matter, tone, and focus, reflective of a transition from carnal to spiritual. Nevertheless, I've known since I was a child that I had a gift for writing so I had assumed that I was just in a *flow* of things. As I grew in understanding, I realized that the Holy Spirit was providing revelation through the words I was recording.

So, what exactly is prayer journaling? Let us begin with what it's not. Although it may contain these elements, it is not simply writing out our prayers verbatim or journaling our thoughts on Scripture. Prayer journaling should be an organic practice that involves creating a written record of our experiences, thoughts, and emotions.

It's important to note that, as Believers, our lives should not be compartmentalized apart from our Heavenly Father. As we grow in faith, we become better equipped to live out Proverbs 3:6 which commands us to acknowledge Him in all of our ways. There is not one situation in our lives that Yah cannot and should not be involved in. Mad at a friend? Tell Him about it. Crushing on someone? Inquire of Him about this person. Dealing with a toxic boss? Get Him on the main line. Did something funny happen? Laugh with Him about it. We will find ourselves quite surprised at how the Holy Spirit will add commentary, sometimes hilarious, to what we are discussing in our private journals. It is another form of communication with the Father.

Prayer journaling can actually be a powerful component of Listening Prayer. It is unique because it can make us feel as if we are speaking, writing, and hearing simultaneously. This is why we may initially confuse the thoughts of the Holy Spirit with our own. For writers, it can indeed feel like a flow as clarity increases in the midst of us documenting our ideas, feelings, and petitions. There are times that prayer journaling can even be reminiscent of speaking in tongues. Sometimes, when we are praying fervently and fall short on words, the Holy Spirit will take over, praying through us and giving us clarity on how to continue praying in our earthly language. We can get in such a zone while writing that we have a similar experience.

Prayer journaling doesn't always fit into a neat box as it is highly individualistic and can contain both intangible and supernatural components. Even on the more practical side, where we journal our thoughts on Scripture, things can become unexpectedly revealing when the Holy Spirit gets involved. This may be difficult to understand if you have not experienced it, but trust me, it's a thing.

While there are generalities that exist in terms of communication, every single person has a unique way of conveying their thoughts both written and verbally. This individuality is even more pronounced when it comes to how we interact with our Heavenly Father. I would encourage readers to begin writing and let your process develop over time. Next, we will explore some of the benefits of prayer journaling and offer tips to begin.

Benefits of Prayer Journaling

Prayer journaling can provide insight on situations we are writing about. Earlier I mentioned the supernatural component to this but there are also practical ways that journaling can provide clarity. First, it helps us to keep an accurate record of ourselves and the situations at hand. The human mind is extremely forgetful. Yah knows this, which is one reason that He often repeats Himself in Scripture. In fact, I had a Sarah moment myself (see Genesis 18:12-15) regarding this very thing. While reading Scripture, I thought to myself, why is Yah always repeating Himself? And why did He answer my thought saying that humans are very forgetful. He also mentioned that He is not confined to our literary norms. Since repetition is usually avoided in writing, I thought to myself, "I guess Yah told me!"

Not only does He repeat Himself, but Yah specifically tells us to **remember** things. Journaling is a powerful tool to help us fulfill this commandment. It is also good for our mental and emotional well being. I can't remember how many times I felt a way about a situation only to go back to my journal and realize that my current perspective differs from what I recorded as happening. An example of this is related to my relocation to Texas. Since I didn't know anyone in Houston, or so I thought, I began questioning what I heard. I thought to myself, *well maybe Yah said Texas and I can just pick which city I want to live in. After all, I at least have a cousin in Dallas.* I went back to my journal and found that it indeed said Houston. Prayer journaling helps us to keep our facts straight when our emotions threaten to deceive us.

Prayer journaling is also a useful method for connecting the dots when we are seeking confirmation on something we've asked of the Most High. We may not fully grasp the *signs* in one or two entries, but when we go back and read several of them, we are better able to recognize a pattern and put things together. We can bet that there will be things that we have forgotten as well.

When done correctly, gratitude is another by-product of prayer journaling. *Counting* and detailing our blessings can be a form of worship that fosters gratefulness. As Believers, many of us underestimate the importance of expressing our thankfulness to the Creator. Yet, from the peace offerings in Leviticus to the Psalmist's repetitive instructions to praise Yah for all that He has done, it is clear that this should be a regular part of our communication with the Most High. In the renewed covenant of the Scripture, we are instructed to include thanksgiving as a part of our petitions. [116]

The Father issues these instructions because, first and foremost, He is worthy, and it is an appropriate response to the One who keeps us in His constant care. However, living from a place of gratitude is helpful to our own well being. Many of us struggle with the tendency to focus on what is going wrong in our lives rather than on what's going well. This is a dangerous habit that can open the door

---

[116] Philippians 4:6

to spiritual attacks on our mental health. Gratitude, on the other hand, is a natural balm for depression. Even those of us with thankful hearts can sometimes use reminders of how Yah has blessed us by way of protection, provision, forgiveness, healing, deliverance, reconciliation, strengthening, comfort, enlightenment, restoration, and the list goes on.

The things we document in our journals help us to recall His faithfulness, intentionality, and care towards us. Personally, my journal entries typically begin with updates and venting sessions but by the close, I'm writing out praises and other loving sentiments to the Father for who He is and how He has moved in my life.

Finally, prayer journaling greatly increases self awareness. A person who can truly see themselves, flaws, and all, has set themselves up for a greater measure of prosperity in every area of their life. Unfortunately, statistics show that only 10-15% of people are self aware, despite 95% claiming to be.[117] Although many of us would like to believe that we are included in that small percentage, chances are that we are not.

Those of us with gifts of discernment are even more prone to fall into this trap. We may presume that because it's easy for us to discern certain things in others, that we have a bird's eye view of ourselves. Romans 12:3 warns about this, encouraging us to be sober minded when it comes to how we view ourselves. Pride and ego work hand in hand to ensure a biased view of our own reflection. The ego has an idea of itself that can blind us to the reality of who we actually are or at least how we are coming off to others. Pride convinces us that we would know if we were off in some area. This

---

[117] Tasha Eurich PhD., "What Self Awareness Really is (and How to Cultivate it)", *Harvard Business Review,* 2018

is why humility is a fruit of the Spirit that must be continually cultivated.

The truth is, whether we fall into that small percentage of the self-aware or not, all of us suffer from blindspots. Prayer journaling will help bring these things to the forefront. There are times when I cringe from reading my past entries, even though at the time that I wrote it, I felt justified in my position. From the vantage point of growth, I am now able to see the error of my ways. This puts my ego on notice that I am not always operating in self awareness, and if it happened then, there is a possibility that it is happening now in some aspect of my life. Blindspots are called blindspots for a reason. We don't know what we don't know. In fact, if we are walking around regularly proclaiming how self-aware we are, we likely still have some ways to go.

The key to increasing self awareness through prayer journaling is honesty. Our prayer journal should be a sacred place for us to express our thoughts and feelings in raw form. We must resist the urge to judge ourselves when we're writing and just write from our core. It is through this that we can expose our hearts which puts us on the path towards correction and healing. We've all heard the saying, "The first step is admitting that you have a problem!" The more honest we are, the greater measure of clarity we will receive. Have you ever had a situation that you were mulling over in your mind, but once you began talking it over with someone else, and actually heard the words coming out of your mouth, you realized how crazy you sounded? While it may not have the immediate effect as when we're verbally expressing ourselves, when we look back on what we wrote, it will provide a clearer perspective.

Through prayer journaling, I have experienced the fact that it is impossible to be honest with anyone if we are not first honest with ourselves. The Most High is no exception to this. We must first admit things to ourselves before we can fix our lips to confess it to the Father. The difference with Him is that He already knows the truth, making it even more asinine to lie to someone who can see the depths of our hearts. We must be as honest as we can for prayer journaling to be effective. There may be times that we look back at former entries and discover that we were not being as honest with ourselves about a situation as we thought. This is the beauty of having a written record to reflect on. Once we get past the initial cringe, we will be grateful to have grown in wisdom and understanding.

As I close out this chapter, I want to provide a few remaining practical tips for prayer journaling:

- **Remember your why.** You are doing this as another form of communication to build intimacy with your Heavenly Father. This will strengthen your spirit man and improve your other relationships.

- **Don't make it a chore.** Try to prayer journal as often as you can but give yourself grace. There are seasons where I journal daily. Other times, a few days or even weeks may pass before I am able to do a complete entry. I try to avoid this from happening too frequently because it can be overwhelming to document all that has happened over a longer period, particularly if you are giving place for the Holy Spirit to be active in your life!

- **Be led by the Spirit.** While you are documenting your life, be sensitive to what you are being led to journal about. Some things I add because I want to remember. Other times, I'm venting or trying to get clarity, and it is often in these instances that the Holy Spirit will provide understanding.

- **Change environments.** Take your journal with you on walks, visits to the park and beach days. Yah speaks to us through nature so feel free to jot down any thoughts that come to you while in the midst of the Creator's canvas.

- **Keep notes.** I give my best effort to spend time with Yah daily. Sometimes it's for hours, other times, it's a half an hour or less. On the days when I am short on time, I still jot down a few notes in my paper journal, or phone, that I can refer to when I have time to write a full entry.

- **Privacy Concerns.** If you are worried about someone reading your private thoughts, you may choose to use an electronic journal. I use a separate email account that is strictly for journaling. This also helps with organization. It allows me to quickly search key words that I remember using when I'm trying to locate something specific. The e-journal also comes in handy when I have a lot to write and it is more practical to type. I have handwritten journals as well, but I tend to use my e-journal when I have some real tea to spill on myself!

In closing, prayer journaling has been an absolute game changer in my spiritual walk. As someone with a shorter attention span and selective memory, I don't think I would have grown to where I am without regularly employing this spiritual discipline. My hope is that you have gathered enough value in this chapter to make prayer journaling a regular part of your journey towards creating greater intimacy with the Most High.

CHAPTER 17

Principles of Bible Study

The Bible is arguably the most controversial and misunderstood group of writings to ever exist. Despite remaining the best-selling book of all time, questions surrounding its origin, translation, and interpretation persist. For the Believer, it is our foundation of faith. It is the very essence of what we believe. At best, it's where we obtain understanding of our Creator and our relationship to Him. At worst, it's where we all get our villain origin stories; we as in us humans, satan, and many who unjustly make Yah to be the bad guy of History.

In some parts of the world, Believers are risking their lives to read the Word of Elohiym. Unfortunately, in the West, many of us view the Bible as optional reading. I'm not sure when this became acceptable, but I can say with certainty that this nonchalant attitude toward Scripture has demonic origins. Unlike many of us, the enemy knows the power of the Word of Yah and he will stop at nothing to keep us from opening it up. I once had a debate with a friend who I was encouraging to read the Word to grow their faith. After a series of exchanges, the person said something to the effect of "all knowledge cannot be contained in the Bible because you cannot contain God." Sensing a circular argument, and what the Bible refers to as vain philosophies,[118] I stopped responding.

Of course, all knowledge is not found in the Bible, but as Believers, it is our starting point. The enemy will work very hard to

---

[118] Colossians 2:8

convince us otherwise. Who wrote the Bible? Who interpreted it? How do we know this? How do we know that? Listen, we are in the last days and it's time to make a decision. While we know that deception is rampant, the Most High is able to preserve the parts of His Word that are necessary for salvation. During slavery times, most of the pages were removed to prevent us from contemplating our true identity, liberation, or even holding our captors accountable. Yet enough information was provided for us to know we had a Messiah that we could place our trust in.

In the hands of a non-Believer, the Bible is just a book. Due to its volume and complexity, its words can be twisted to support almost any narrative. However, in the possession of a born again Believer, it is more valuable than any earthly treasure. Its pages contain a history of our faith, an explicative love letter, and an instruction manual from our Creator.

When the enemy is not distracting us with endless accusations surrounding the Bible's credibility or relativity, then he'll seduce us into believing it's too difficult to understand. When that fails, he'll ensure that we're too tired or our children are extra needy when it's time to get into the Word. The notifications on our phones will be incessant and our mothers will just so happen to call as soon as we've sat down to read.

These tactics are not limited to reading, as any form of consumption of the Word can be attacked. Have you ever been listening to a message and when the speaker starts reading the Scripture aloud you notice your attention waning? I actually experienced this years ago while watching a YouTube video. Thankfully the messenger was wise enough to call it out. She literally said that it's a spirit tempting you to click off the video once a prolonged reading of Scripture ensues. Since then, I have been vigilant to not allow that to happen, even if I am already familiar with the passages being read.

I'm not interested in giving the enemy too much attention, but again, Scripture warns us to be aware of his devices. Therefore, if you don't recall much else from this section I humbly implore you to remember this: If you do not have a desire to read the Word, or even if you do but there is something hindering you, you are experiencing spiritual warfare. Please know that it is not enough to simply acknowledge this fact. It is our responsibility to pray and fast if need be for strength to persevere. There will be no excuse good enough when we are called to give an account of our lives and Yah asks us why we did not prioritize His Word.

With that said, we won't address whether or not the Bible is a worthy investment of our time. If you haven't noticed, which if you have not been reading your Bible you may have very well missed this fun fact, the end times events that were prophesied from long ago are manifesting with increasing speed. This requires us all to make choices about what is most important. Note that this is not a "how to" on how to read the Bible but rather to communicate the necessity of it for those wishing to have an intimate relationship with the Most High.

While there will be some practical take-aways, this chapter is primarily intended to be a source of motivation. There are countless resources out there on how to read the Bible, but the best advice I can give is to pray for wisdom, understanding, and get started. If there is something you're having trouble comprehending, ask the Holy Spirit for clarity. We are not just nearing the end times, we are here. Deception and confusion is rapidly increasing and this is not the time to be solely dependent on man regardless of his or her title.

Here, I am pleading with you to not allow yourself to be deceived. There is no getting around reading the Word of Yah. I'm not saying that it is impossible to have any type of growth sans Scripture, but it will result in us being wildflowers rather than well dressed fruitful branches of the Vine[119]. We will lack discernment, understanding, and our ignorance will have us blowing in the direction of every new doctrine[120] thus putting our souls at risk. Instead, let us adhere to the instruction of the Word which says to study to show ourselves approved.[121]

In the following section, we'll discuss five principles that will provide a fresh perspective on Bible study and how to increase its effectiveness.

Reading to Know Him

It is my genuine belief that once we begin to view the Bible as a way to know our Creator, we will experience a life changing paradigm shift. This world has a way of dulling us to things that we should be interested in. Truth be told, Yah is more interesting than anyone or anything and we should want to know our Elohiym. He is the Ancient of Days with no beginning or end. The Creator of all, who knows all that there was, all that there is, and all that there will ever be. Yet in all that He is, which our words cannot contain, He also desires to be known and intimately acquainted with those that He made in His image.

To get the full benefit of reading Scripture, we must first pivot our mindsets away from ourselves. Being that we were created for His pleasure, our existence should revolve around Him. If our

---

[119] John 15:1-5
[120] Ephesians 4:14
[121] 2 Timothy 2:15

perspective on reading Scripture is rooted in receiving blessings or avoiding hell, then we have missed it. To know Yah is to love Him. To love Him is to obey Him. Obedience through the power of the Messiah brings about both earthly and eternal rewards. In short, blessings will surely come, as will our seat in heavenly places, but I would encourage love for our Elohiym to remain the driving factor for all that we do.

To credit my friend from earlier, I must note that as we grow in our faith we will begin to know our Elohiym for ourselves, outside the pages of the Bible. We will go from viewing Him as an ancient, distant Elohiym that worked wonders in the early world, to One who is active and personally invested in our daily lives. Scripture will always serve as our "control group" so to speak. It helps us to accurately measure if what we are experiencing is truly our Heavenly Father or of another spirit. The Bible provides the framework for us to grow in our knowledge and understanding of Him. Is the way in which we are experiencing Him aligning with what we already know about Him from Scripture? Does it fall in step with His character as defined in the Word? From what we've read about our Messiah, is it something that He would do or approve of? Sometimes we just have to take it back to the basics of WWJD!

To do this, it is necessary to have an accurate understanding of Him. It can not be based on the traditions of man which suggest vague notions such as "God is love" meaning anything goes as long as it's done in *love*. Many of us do not even understand what love is. We have projected this age's penchant for inclusivity and tolerance onto an Elohiym who is actually very exclusive and intolerant of the things that He Himself defines as abominable. The Most High says that He chastens those that He loves. So if there is never any conviction or refinement occurring in our faith walk, then it is fair to ask which god are we serving? Studying the Word of Yah helps us to avoid this common pitfall by truly helping us to know our King.

Eliminating Deception & Building Faith

Reading the Word eliminates confusion, brings clarity and safeguards us from deception. There are many controversial topics in faith-based communities that need not be. For instance, why is abortion debatable if Yah explicitly stated in the Ten Commandments that killing is wrong? Why is fornication excused because it occurs between a man and a woman? The Scripture specifically addresses fornication in 1 Corinthians 6:9. Spoiler alert: it says not to be deceived, fornicators will NOT enter the Kingdom of Elohiym. It also speaks to it in other places i.e. the woman at the well with the six *non-husbands.* [122]

Perhaps because this sin has become so rampant in our society, we believe that the Scripture would have spoken more about it if Yah really didn't want people having sexual relations outside of marriage. That sounds about right for a typical lie that satan would plant into our minds. Nevertheless, we must remember who the Scriptures were written to and for. Whether they always adhered to it or not, our Hebrew ancestors knew darn well that we were not supposed to be having sex outside of marriage. As it is said in our community, what's understood doesn't have to be said.

This is why it is important that we not only read Yah's Word but we do so with the intent of knowing His will and doing it. This will help us operate off biblical principles concerning things that the Scriptures may not have specifically addressed. For example, 1 Thessalonians 4:3-4 says, ***"For this is the will of Elohiym, even***

---

[122] John 4:16-18

your sanctification, that ye should abstain from fornication: That every one of you should know how to possess his vessel in sanctification and honor. Not in passionate lust, even as the other nations which know not Elohiym." How is masturbation synonymous with the principle of sexual purity that our Elohiym calls us to in this verse? What is holy and honorable about this act? The Scripture doesn't tell us not to eat our waste but we can derive from Yah's instructions regarding bodily cleanliness[123] and the dietary laws[124] that this would be inappropriate.

We must be careful about the things we justify because it is not explicitly stated in Scripture, particularly when it comes to ourselves. Romans 14 tells us how to manage things that are not forbidden in Scripture that we do not feel a particular conviction about. It tells us to enjoy our liberty privately as not to be a stumbling block to those who may be of weaker faith. We must allow others the Elohiym-given freedom to decide that for themselves. But when it comes to our own souls, we need to be sober minded and sensitive to the Holy Spirit which will most certainly tell us when we have stepped out of bounds.

Confusion is a gateway to deception and deception separates us from the Most High. It lays the foundation for a distorted view of Him, of ourselves, and His expectations. Let's look back at mother Eve's encounter with the serpent. He doesn't just bring the forbidden fruit and tell her to eat of it. He starts by bringing confusion by leading her to question what Yah actually *said* about eating the fruit. We give Eve a hard time, but the truth is the enemy is still doing the same exact thing today. Yah says one thing, often verbatim, and then the enemy asks us "Well, is that what He really

___

[123] Deuteronomy 23:10-14
[124] Leviticus 11

meant?" He then cunningly whispers, "Well, this is a special circumstance…surely Yah wouldn't want a victim of rape to keep a child."

When possible, we are much better off using wisdom in avoiding these situations in the first place. Wisdom also means living righteous lives. While being with a stranger at a hotel at 3 am does not excuse any form of assault, does it truly demonstrate the wisdom and righteousness that the Scripture calls us to? This may be counter cultural and even triggering, but a degree of accountability in such situations is actually Biblical. [125] This is why we read it. We need not govern ourselves by the norms of this wicked realm where everything is inverted. We are citizens of the Kingdom of the Most High and intimately acquainting ourselves with His Word offers a measure of protection and prosperity that the world cannot.

When situations occur that are out of our control, it is best to take it to the Father and ask for help. He is willing and able. We may not see a way out but that is when Yah does His best work. It is up to us to have the necessary faith to trust Him in all circumstances. Life is full of nuance, but it's better to err on the side of what the Word actually says. Reading it brings clarity by defining His instructions and what to do when we fail or find ourselves affected by the failure of others.

It's also imperative that we have an established relationship, rooted in obedience, before we start running to Yah in times of trouble. I am not saying that we cannot or should not go to the Father in our time of need, regardless of the relationship status. Yah is merciful and the situation may be exactly what is needed to bring us into true repentance and deeper relationship with Him.

---

[125] Deuteronomy 22:23-26

However, in these cases we must manage our expectations. After living in rebellion for years, or even worse, treating our Elohiym as an afterthought,[126] life happens and we throw ourselves at the foot of the throne. We plead for mercy and make promises that we may or may not keep. If He doesn't answer in the way we expect, bitterness and resentment toward Him begin to take root in our hearts. This is an unfair, unreasonable, juvenile mindset.

Let's say, you yourself had a child who you made your best efforts to parent with love, care, and discipline. Yet, this child refused to have anything to do with you or the wholesome ways in which you raised them. All of a sudden, the defiant child who you can't remember the last time you've heard from, is in great need and expecting you, the parent, to come to their rescue. Will you? Probably. It's your child. However, the child having lived in prolonged disobedience and estrangement, should in no way feel entitled to your help.

Thankfully, in many cases, Yah is gracious, desiring for all men to be reconciled to Him. Yet, there are times that allowing us to endure consequences for our actions is indeed a veiled act of mercy. The Bible is filled with countless examples of times when Yah brought deliverance to terrible situations or in His sovereignty, allowed some things to work out for good in the end. They serve as sources of counsel, comfort, and hope. Equally important, they prevent us from placing limits on the Most High in terms of what He can and cannot do. These ancestral chronicles are there to teach and remind us about the Elohiym that we serve. Read them and be encouraged!

---

[126] Revelation 3:15-17

<u>Understanding: Prescriptive vs Descriptive</u>

Reading the Scriptures with understanding is paramount because without it, we will have a perverted view of the One whom we are seeking to know. Much can be learned about our Elohiym through how He instructs His people in the Word. We also get to know Him by observing how He responds to them as they navigate things common to all such as family, money, community, etc.

This is why it's imperative to know the difference between prescription and description. The former is a means of instruction while the latter is simply providing information on the people and situations being reported. We often speak in error due to the belief that because something is recorded in Scripture, it means that the Most High condones it. But we deal with a merciful Elohiym who bears with a lot of man's ways due to our nature. For instance, we know that Yah hates divorce,[127] but in some instances, it has been permitted because of the hardness of man's hearts.[128]

Yah is all knowing which means that He considers nuance. Therefore, in some instances, rather than create hardline boundaries that, depending on the situation, may cause more harm than good, He instead sets guidelines. We can look to practices such as slavery and polygamy as examples of this. It is not the Most High's perfect will that any of His people be enslaved. However, because we live in a fallen world, there are times where it comes to that. In His wisdom, He has provided laws that guide the master and protect the servant.

We also know that Yah's preference would be for one man to have one wife. Yet, there are circumstances such as the greater goal

---

[127] Malachi 2:16
[128] Matthew 19:8

of increasing population or making sure that none of His daughters were left uncovered that He allowed a man to have multiple wives. Although there were governing rules for polygamy, Scripture shows us how these unions were still filled with plenty of unnecessary turmoil.

The Father can be very hands on. Other times, He allows man's will to drive History while setting parameters to keep things within acceptable limits according to His sovereignty. As His creation, we would be wise to align with His original intention as much as possible. We do this by reading the Word without our own agenda, but instead with sober discernment and the intent of knowing Him.

The Role of the Holy Spirit & Wisdom

Despite its popularity, there is nothing common about the Bible. It is a living Word, which means it brings forth life in those who read and adhere to its words. The Scripture being "living" also means that the Most High can supernaturally use it as a means to speak to us today. This is not to be taken in a general sense as any literate person can open up the Bible and comprehend that lying and stealing is wrong. I am saying that Yah can use thousands of years old words to speak to our personal affairs of today. The Scripture alone may not give you the exact specifics on how to handle modern issues but it will give you timeless wisdom to apply to the situation. Similar to prayer journaling, it can be difficult to understand if you haven't experienced it.

Likewise, it should be understood that the Bible is for Believers and for those coming to faith. Individuals who fall within either of these groups are reading with the intent to understand and apply the words to their lives. The Most High knows who is reading in genuine search of Him. This is important to remember as we discuss the role of the Holy Spirit that aids us in our discernment of Scripture.

Recently, the Holy Spirit revealed to me that any truth that we learn from others, be it through direct teaching or by proxy, is tainted because it has *them* attached to it. We do not simply learn the information, we absorb it within the context of the teacher's biases, opinions, world view, culture, experiences, hang-ups, interpretation, level of understanding and so forth. As I pondered on this, I realized that even when we learn directly from the Holy Spirit, it is still received through our own personal filter of the same. Of course we all believe that we are teaching and receiving pure truth, but that's just not the case. The Apostle Paul, who wrote much of the New Testament, speaks to this inevitable lack of understanding in 1 Corinthians 13:12 as he writes, ***"For now we see in a mirror dimly, but then face to face. Now I know in part; then I shall know fully, even as I have been fully known."***

We must be vigilant in seeking Yah to receive truth in the most purest form. The Holy Spirit also showed me that this purification of truth is not something that just happens, rather than, as with all things, it is a process occurring over time. It is continuous as we move through the various cycles of life, learning and unlearning. Remaining grounded in both the written and living Word, the person of Yahusha Ha'Mashiach, allows us to tread fearlessly as we are led into deeper waters. [129]

It is our responsibility to be aware of these things and proceed accordingly. Practically speaking, that means being a clean vessel to receive understanding of Yah's Word. We cannot expect to grieve the Holy Spirit and receive proper revelation of Scripture. Sin will

---

[129] John 4:10

most definitely pollute our understanding as justifications, concessions, and compromised mindsets will convolute even the most straightforward Biblical truths. This calls for us to die to self, de-center our fellow man, and center Yah.

This is not to say that we cannot learn from one another or from those who have been gifted with teaching abilities. But we should do so with the understanding that we are primarily responsible for our own souls. As maturing Believers, we should be taking our inquiries regarding Scripture to the Holy Spirit. When these same questions are later presented to teachers or come up in conversation with other Believers, we pray for confirmation regarding their response.

In my experience, answers from others, whether it be teachers or laymen, are typically confirmation of what the Holy Spirit has already told me. This also guards our hearts from idolatry that can tempt us to exalt man, making *him* our source, rather than Yah. Additionally, it can temper pride in others who may carry certain titles or may just simply be more knowledgeable than us. We all should be following after the example of the Bereans who, when Paul came with what they perceived to be new doctrine, they searched the Scriptures to make sure that what he said lined up.[130]

With us living in such a contentious society, I do feel the need to make this disclaimer. We don't always have to challenge someone with another perspective in the moment or even make a proclamation that we are "testing the Spirit." It's reasonable to ask clarifying questions to make sure we are accurately comprehending what is being stated. There are situations where it may be necessary

---

[130] Acts 17:10-11

to address things immediately, particularly for the sake of those present who may be less experienced in the faith.

However, it is perfectly acceptable to take our difference in perspective to the Most High privately. Give the Holy Spirit time to respond as the answer may not come that day or the next. Sometimes things play out in a way that Yah allows a situation to give us a real life example of the answer. Whenever the answer comes, we can return to our brother, sister, or teacher and the two of us can reason with one another. In Hebrew culture, this is a part of what is referred to as midrash.

Contextual Understanding

Regarding the topic of Hebrew, cultural context will also aid us in our understanding of Scripture. It is imperative that we do not insert a Western worldview onto Yah's Word. If you are reading this book, you are likely living in a modern Western culture. This means that we, as 21st century English speaking people, are attempting to understand a text that is over 2000 years old, written in a different language, from an ancient culture that we are far removed from. It is akin to a Black American writer, authoring a historical and spiritual book that later finds itself in the hands of Russians in 7000 A.D.

I realize that's a wild analogy, especially given that I highly doubt we'll be here that long. Nevertheless, my aim was to demonstrate the extreme shift in culture, language, and time that would severely impact the reader's ability to accurately discern what is being communicated. Not to mention, the dark forces that are at work to ensure that the truth of Yahuah's Word does not come through in its purest form.

Aside from relying on the Holy Spirit, it is up to us to dig deeper. This means we take the time to look up the original meaning of words written in Hebrew. We must also learn to understand Scripture from the mindset of the people that the book was written by so that our comprehension is robust. This may lead us to explore some secular historical accounts of events which can both corroborate and provide another frame of reference to what we are reading in Scripture.

For instance, during Covid, I attended a women's Bible Study in Houston at what I believe was an evangelical church. I was new to the area and a neighbor who I'd become friendly with invited me. The topic was the book of Esther and the teacher, who also taught at a local college, had us read accounts of Flavius Josephus, a Roman-Jewish historian. Among religious scholars, his research is regarded as a primary source, outside of the Bible, of information regarding Israelite history.

I read the materials that the teacher provided, but somehow, I *stumbled* upon some other writings of Mr. Josephus where both the Egyptians and Israelites were described as black people. At the time, the Holy Spirit had already been leading me down a path of certain truths and this was just another link in an unraveling chain of lies. Let it be noted that I was not seeking this piece of information at all. I was genuinely studying the life of Queen Esther and was innocently digging deeper out of curiosity about the political climate and other surrounding circumstances of her time.

We would be shocked where the Holy Spirit will take us when we take the initiative to go beyond the bare minimum. When we make time for Scripture, layers will begin to unfold like an onion. A study Bible will link topical verses together and we can find ourselves reading from three different books in one sitting. With patient diligence, revelation will ensue and we will begin to see how much we have been missing by limiting our reading of Scripture to the verse of the day from our daily devotional. The understanding that we can know Yah for ourselves, just like our ancestors in the Bible, starts to become a reality. We no longer have to solely depend on what others have taught us about our Elohiym. Even the things that we learned that were correct will now be validated in real time.

As the Holy Spirit leads us into all truth, a separation will take place that we must be courageous enough to withstand. We will grow increasingly intolerant of religious rhetoric and dogma, and find ourselves praying to deal graciously with those who perpetuate it out of the ignorance that we once partook in. If we are laying the foundation for the fruit of the Spirit[131] to be functional within us, then this will be a tremendously humbling process. We will realize that even with our heightened understanding, what we don't know still heavily outweighs what we do know. Through it all, a quiet confidence will permeate our souls as we receive the peace that comes from having an intimate relationship with the Creator. Most importantly, this is something that can never be taken from us. Should they burn every Bible in sight, the living treasure that we have already stored up in ourselves will continue to work wonders.

"Seek ye Yahuah while He may be found..." —Isaiah 55:6

---

[131] Galatians 5:22-23

CHAPTER 18

Meditation Part 1
Principles of Meditation

As I began writing this chapter, Psalms 19:14 came to mind: *"Let the words of my mouth, and the meditation of my heart, be acceptable in Your sight, O Yahuah, my strength and my Redeemer."* In this verse, *meditation* is associated with the heart. We use the term *heart* to describe what is obscure, our underlying motives, as opposed to what can be tangibly observed; our actions. Such phrases include *heart posture*, having a *heart* for something, *God knows my heart*, and so on. In present times, meditation typically corresponds to the mind. This led me to question the original meaning of the word *heart* when used in the verse above.

Consulting the Strong's Concordance I discovered that the word in Hebrew for this concept was *leb* which encompasses the inner man, mind, will, and heart. This implies that while we tend to make a distinction between the heart and the mind, at least in this occurrence, the Scripture does not. At minimum, they are intrinsically linked in a way that they can be used interchangeably.

An unknown ancient philosopher once wrote, "Watch your thoughts, they become words; watch your words, they become actions; watch your actions; they become habits; watch your habits, they become character; watch your character, for it becomes your destiny." It doesn't take more than our natural senses to discern the truth in this statement. But where do thoughts come from? Does desire play a role? Does one precede the other? This leads us to a necessary exploration of the distinction between the two. While both desire and thought may originate from the same place, the *leb*, they can exist independently, influence one another, and also be subject to external forces.

Desire & Thought

At a base level, desire is not always accompanied by conscious thought. It can simply be a natural inclination towards something. Beyond our instincts are the desires given to us by the Most High to bring forth the manifestation of our destinies. Let's consider Psalm 37:4 that says, ***"Delight yourself also in Yahuah; and He shall give you the desires of your heart."*** This verse is often erroneously interpreted to mean that Yah will give us whatever we want. A better understanding would be that the desires are actually given to us *by* Yah. Due to our brokenness, we are often unable to maintain our desires in a healthy way which can lead us down the path of lust and idolatry.

This is why there is a need for us to have our desires purified. A clue to the purification process is given in the first half of Psalms 37:4 where it tells us to *delight* ourselves in Yahuah. The Strong's Concordance indicates that the word delight comes from the root word **anag** which means soft, pliable, with effeminate undertones. This makes sense when we consider the posture that a woman has towards her husband. We could also compare it to Israel being married to Yahuah and Yahusha coming for His bride. When we as a people or individuals have a *leb* that is soft and pliable towards Elohiym, it is open to His leadership and will prepare us to receive what we desire. Having our desires purified entails us giving them over to Elohiym so that when He returns them, they are no longer primarily viewed as a means to get our needs met. The desires are now rooted in glorifying Him and serving others.

As for us, we will be blessed by both default and intention. It is a universal law that our generosity will be returned to us even if not in the exact form that it was given. Our Elohiym also rewards those who serve from a pure place, and because it is impossible to out give Him, we will always receive more than what we put out. This brings forth both the fulfillment and fruit of the two greatest commandments[132] in a beautiful way that only He can.

When it comes to our relationship with Yah, desire is indeed a crucial starting point. It is what attracts Him and positions us to begin our life with Him as our focal point. Yet, it is only the beginning. Enter in *thought*, which is part of the conscious process needed for our desires to materialize. As with desire, our thoughts do not always originate with us. This realization can take us on a journey to better discern the voice of the Holy Spirit from our own.

However, just as the enemy wishes to pervert our desires, he is also the author of intrusive thoughts. Consider a situation where we are experiencing a great deal of mental, emotional, or even physical distress over an extended period of time. Naturally, we would long to be free of this suffering. As a result of this desire, thoughts of suicide can begin to manifest. This is a satanic attempt to take advantage of our vulnerability during a time when we are finding it difficult to cope. If we were able to see beyond our current state of agony, we would know that we don't actually want to die. We really just want to be free from the pain that we are in at the moment. Just as satan will use our desires against us, he will also send thoughts that steer us toward self destruction.

---

[132] Matthew 22:36-40

Our own thoughts are linked to how we process information and knowledge to bring forth a desired end. Measuring our thoughts against Scripture and our lived experiences form the basis for wisdom and knowledge. Yahuah encourages us to ask for the former[133] and says that His people are destroyed for lack of the latter.[134] Notice that nothing is mentioned about the heart, how His people felt, or what their intentions were. Remember, Uzzah? He was one of King David's men chosen to carry the Ark of the Covenant which was synonymous with the very presence of Yah. When the oxen that were carrying it began to stumble, Uzzah reached out to steady the Ark and was immediately stricken dead.[135] We can all agree that his heart was in the right place, but he indeed perished out of ignorance.

Maintaining our Leb

Both desire and thought must be made whole, allowing them to work harmoniously to execute that which brings forth the will of the Most High. This requires a *leb* that is purified and filled with both wisdom and knowledge. The sticking point for many is that this is not something that happens automatically once we *accept* Mashiach. There is an underlying tone in the faith that all we have to do is believe because the Messiah "paid it all". The reality is that we have a part to play in the maintenance of our leb. Perhaps in the perfect world, such as the one that Yah originally created, it would be easier to just float as you ate from your perfect garden, with your perfect spouse, and walked with your perfect Elohiym in the cool of the day.

---

[133] James 1:5
[134] Hosea 4:6
[135] Samuel 6:3-7

Unfortunately, we no longer exist in a paradisiacal vacuum. The world has been turned over to dark forces and we must fight to stay above water. It is a curious thing that this concept seems to only apply when it comes to a relationship with the Elohiym of the Bible. Any married person will testify to how much work it is to sustain a healthy commitment. We also know what it takes to be successful in our respective occupations. A measure of labor is even required when it comes to our hobbies. No one learns to play the piano or excels in martial arts without a significant amount of effort. It's almost as if when we come into the faith, the basic laws of nature vanish.

When work is considered, it is usually centered on that which is outwardly focused such as evangelism, feeding the homeless, serving in our church/assembly, etc. While these things are necessary, if they are done with a leb that is not intimately acquainted with its Creator, then it is all done in vain as it pertains to our souls.[136] The work that I am referring to has to do with our inner man, our minds to be precise. Thankfully in regards to any work, Messiah tells us that His yoke is easy and His burden is light.[137] This means that when we are postured correctly, He does the heavy lifting.

However, there are some things that we must pick up for ourselves and of utmost importance is the helmet of salvation.[138] This deals with the mind because not only is it a part of our leb, but it is a gateway to it. There is a two way flow to and from the leb and a closed one is not functional. No where in Scripture does it instruct us to be closed-hearted or closed-minded. Instead, Proverbs 4:23

---

[136] Matthew 7:22-23
[137] Matthew 11:30
[138] Ephesians 6:17

tells us, ***"Above all else, guard your heart, for everything you do flows from it."*** Isn't this reminiscent of the ancient philosopher's words summarized? As always, the Most High is lightyears ahead of anyone who thinks himself wise.

Ultimately, our leb is how we connect to Elohiym so it is essential that it be pure, filled with knowledge, wisdom, and guarded. In this chapter, the *work* that is involved in maintaining this is meditation.

What is Meditation?

In modern times, meditation is frequently associated with new age practices. Typically, the goal is to remain present in the moment as the mind is emptied of all thought. Before I knew better, I made several unsuccessful attempts at this. I have the type of brain that enjoys taking random trips to ponder everything from what happened in 1987 to what I'll be having for dinner that night.

For Messianic Believers, this is not our practice. The literal definition of meditation is to think deeply or carefully about something. Unsurprisingly, this is the opposite of what is commonly taught. Remember that the rulers of this world labor tirelessly to push principles that are contrary to the Creator's. The phrase *new age* in itself is deceptive because there is nothing new but rather a perverted counterfeit of a principle, law, or design that Yah has already established. So for Believers, we do not need to seek to have a blank mind as a means of meditation. In this writing, the focus of our meditation will be on our Creator, His Word, the personage of our Messiah along with the things listed in Philippians 4:1. This is instrumental in the conditioning of our leb or even what Scripture refers to as the renewing of our minds.

How Meditation Renews our Minds (Lebs)

A renewed mind goes hand in hand with being a born again Believer. If we profess to be new creatures in Mashiach but possess the same leb as pre-conversion, then what exactly has changed? When we sincerely humble ourselves before Yah in repentance, accept the Messiah as the penalty for our sins, and agree to live a life pleasing to Him going forward, a shift takes place within us. Some changes may be immediate while others will be a part of an on-going deliverance and refining process. However, what will manifest quickly is a desire and willingness to live righteously along with the power of the Holy Spirit to begin doing so. It is then our job to move forward in obedience as the old man dies, allowing more room for that power to totally transform us over time.

It's worth reiterating that transformation does not mean turning into religious clones that parrot traditions of man being passed off as doctrine. That is the form of godliness that lacks power as referenced in 2 Timothy 3:5. We are seeking the type of power that restores us back to the original version of ourselves that the Creator imagined before placing us in our mother's womb. It is us in our highest and purest form: unique, set-apart, righteous, powerful and functional according to Yah's design!

Metacognition & Thought Transformation

"For as he thinks in his heart, so is he.." - Proverbs 23:7

When the Holy Spirit brought this Scripture to mind, I erroneously thought it to be in the New Testament. I had confused it with Yahusha's words in Matthew 5 which expand on this principle. There He tells us that even our lustful thoughts make us adulterers and those who harbor unrighteous anger towards their brethren will be judged just as will those who commit murder.[139] It's interesting because earlier we spoke on how the Messiah holds us to a higher standard than the Torah which focuses on outward expressions of righteousness. But even here in the days of King Solomon, we are being shown the importance of having our inner man sanctified.

I have seen several versions of the philosopher's words that say: change your thoughts, change your habits, change your life. Again, this is reflective of the ubiquitous law implying a direct correlation between what we deposit and what we receive. Therefore, what, how, and when we think about our Creator, and all things related to His Kingdom, will have a major impact on our leb. Are these thoughts Scripturally sound? Are we thinking soberly or through the lens of someone other than the Holy Spirit? Do we only think about the things of Yah when we worship on the weekend, during our morning devotional or are our thoughts centered on Him throughout the day? Questions like these steer our metacognition into alignment with Scripture which encourages us to keep our eyes on Yah.

Discernment & Faith

Having a mind centered on the Most High will sharpen our discernment. The way that currency inspectors check for a counterfeit is not so much in studying fake money. Instead, they familiarize themselves with the authentic bills so well that they can immediately detect a knock off. It works the same way in the spiritual realm. We want to get to the point that we are so intimately

---

[139] Matthew 5:21-22, 27-28

acquainted with our Father that we can tell when something is of Him and when it's not.[140]

We will not only possess the ability to discern falsity, but we'll also begin to see His hand constantly at work around us. This builds faith in the reality that we serve a living Elohiym who is near and active. It also leads to gratefulness as it is a great source of joy when we begin to see Scripture come to life in real time. Verses that speak to *"all things working for our good"* or how *"every good gift and every perfect gift is from above"*[141] are no longer just words on a page. They are personal and we become legitimate witnesses to the goodness of Yah. It takes humility to see Yah in the little things. People often mock the elderly, or those deemed *extra religious*, for constantly praising Yah for everything. Yet, when it is coming from the mouth of one who is walking in true fellowship with Him, we can be assured that person has something that many lack.

My prayer partner once attended a fancy gala where she wore press on nails to complete her look. She texted me during the event telling me how one of the nails kept popping off and she would lose it, but then added, "all praises to the Most High I keep finding it." That was truly one of the funniest praises I've ever heard in my life. It was all the more humorous because I know she was dead serious. And for that reason, the Father made sure that His daughter was not walking around the event looking tacky! That may seem like an odd thing to include here, but my hope is to give a glimpse of what a life of intimacy with the Father can look like. He is not just there to bless us with families, jobs, and homes. He cares about the little things that we care about as well!

---

[140] John 10:27
[141] Romans 8:28, James 1:17

Physical & Spiritual Healing

We've heard the phrase "we are spirit beings having a human experience." It is implied that the human part is referring to our physicality and the material world around us. We also know that should our bodies become incapacitated to the point of death, then our spirit man can longer exist in this realm, as by the law of Yah, the human spirit does not just get to hang around on earth without a physical casing. On the other hand, we know that our leb can become so damaged that it can actually have a negative impact on our bodies. Thus the two parts make up an inseparable whole that the Scripture calls our temple.

Most adults have a general idea of how to care for their physical bodies by way of diet, exercise, lifestyle choices and even being mindful of environmental threats. However, because of our Western mindset, we tend to fall short on making the connection to the effect these things actually have on our leb. Even more so, we are unaware of how the immaterial "food" that we consume can affect our inner man. While this is obviously not the case in every instance, mental and emotional negativity such as bitterness, unforgiveness, and resentment can manifest as sickness in the body. It is also a proven scientific fact that brain chemistry can be affected by our thoughts. An ongoing depressive state can actually damage our neurons. In severe cases, the damage can be so extensive that a temporary medicinal remedy may be needed to get a person over the initial hump while they build themselves back up spiritually to a place where they can receive complete deliverance.

This is an example of the intricate relationship between our physical man and our leb. Just as things manifest first in the spirit realm before the physical, so it is the same in our bodies. As a reminder, we are speaking of universal principles that transcend religious doctrine. As it relates to meditation, focusing on Yah, His Word, and all things associated with His Kingdom has the same effect of what secular society calls *positive thinking*. Even the world has the wisdom to understand that gratitude treats depression. With that being the case, how much more powerful of an effect will Truth filled with grace, love, hope, and wisdom have on our leb?

Meditating on the things of Yah gives us the precious gift of an eternal perspective. This is the ability to see beyond our circumstances and focus on a time that we know, without a shadow of a doubt, will be filled with endless joy. Although things may look terrible at the moment, we know that the Most High will eventually deliver us. We are mature enough to understand that while He may not be causing it, He is allowing it. Our job is to find out why and pass the test, while allowing our hope in Elohiym to sustain us.

Many years ago, during a season of depression, I found myself going through the motions of everyday life while centering my thoughts on Heaven. In the midst of it, I didn't know when the season was going to end, but I knew if nothing else, I had eternity to look forward to. That may seem extreme, but sometimes we have to fight for our minds the best way we know how to at the time. My friend and I now look back and laugh about my strategy, but it was effective!

We have spoken at length on the leb because it is what we use to connect with our Creator which is the basis of this book. It is understood that our temple is composed of two parts: flesh and spirit. The wellness of one affects the other. I find myself humbled by individuals who, while enduring immense physical suffering, continue to press forward in faith, even harder than some able bodied people. It is certainly a measure of grace given. Meanwhile, I can hardly press through a headache to pray. Thankfully, the ability to connect with our Creator is something that can never be taken away from us, even if we must do so silently from within our leb.

Nevertheless, we should do all that we can to maintain the physical part of our temples. A typo brought it to my attention that there is only a one letter difference between meditation and medication. Essentially, meditation is a means to keep our lebs healthy, acting as a guard against anything that would hinder the intimacy with the Most High that we desire.

CHAPTER 19

Meditation Part 2: Practical Application

Meditation moves us beyond simply *reading and doing* to giving deeper consideration to what we're consuming along with our response to it. It allows us to take inventory of our thought life, challenging us to examine our line of thinking, along with why we perceive things the way that we do. Our brains, likened to massive computers, were not given for the sole purpose of controlling our bodies and communicating. Even an android can be programmed to do that so surely Yah expects more of intelligent beings created in His image. He has, in fact, elevated us above all living things on the earth[142], giving us a high level of consciousness with the ability to reason. Apart from natural instinct, it is the desire of the inner man that moves the brain to give the signal for us to act. Therefore, the inner man, or what we have been referring to as the leb, must be set on the things of Yah for those actions to be aligned with His will.

In the following section, we will focus on the three aspects of meditation listed in the previous chapter. This list is not exhaustive, as there are always deeper levels to go in Yah, but it is meant to serve as a solid starting point.

Meditating on Yah and His Word

Meditation plays a role in elevating the reading of Scripture to actually studying. It is time spent turning the Word over and over in

---

[142] Genesis 1:26-28

our minds. During this contemplative state, we may consider what the passages tell us about the personality or character of the Most High. In the chapter on Bible Study, we discussed how reading Scripture is a way to get to know our Elohiym. Meditation heightens this. It can be the difference in knowing about Him versus actually knowing Him.

Using the example of Uzzah from earlier, we can see that the man knew enough about Yah to know that the Ark of the Covenant was holy and it would be a shameful thing for it to fall to the ground. However, He did not know the Creator enough to understand that He is too holy to be touched by human hands nor does He need our help to stay afloat. Initially, Uzzah's judgment seemed harsh, but the more I got to know the Most High, the more I saw how much of an insult his actions were. This is an example of how truly meditating on what we're reading and comparing it to what we know about Yah can bring us to an intimate knowledge of Him.

As we meditate on certain Scriptures, we may reflect on the ways in which it confirms what we already know. If we perceive a contradiction, it becomes an invitation to take it to the Father in prayer for clarity. We might also consider what lessons we can extrapolate to apply to our own lives and those that we are in fellowship with. Being that the Scriptures say that nothing is new under the sun, we may contemplate what these verses tell us about the world around us. Often, the Holy Spirit will lead us in a line of questioning and the meditative state postures us to receive revelation. Should answers not come in that moment, we can always use the questions to dive deeper into study at another time.

When we spend time in the Word, it's not for us to just read and go on about our day. We would be amazed at how pondering Yah's Word, no matter how ancient the verse, can allow us to glean a truth that is somehow applicable today. It may even just take us into greater revelation of the Creator, Himself which is always a precious gift.

Meditating on Messiah

Reflecting on Yahusha's sacrifice, which makes way for us to be reconciled to the Father, conditions our hearts to remain humble. Without His bloodshed, there is neither forgiveness nor redemption for sin. There is no us without Him which is why we are preparing to become one with Him as His bride. These thoughts should stir up enduring gratefulness in us as we honor the Most High for His selfless plan.

As written in Chapter 14, *Prayers of Refinement,* centering the Messiah in our thoughts positions us for perpetual refinement. He is the standard and any comparisons should ultimately be made to Him. How are our ways aligned with His teachings and the principles of His lifestyle? Remembering that His ultimate goal was always to do the will of the Father should be an anchoring thought as we endeavor to follow His example.

Many Believers want the glorious aspects of the Messiah's life. We want to be called Rabbi, Bishop, Apostle, Pastor, etc. We want to perform miracles, give prophetic words, and be renowned for our work in the Kingdom. But, are we willing to fast like Yahusha and spend copious amounts of time at the feet of the Father being taught by the Holy Spirit? Are we willing to humble ourselves to the extent that He did? Are we willing to put earthly treasures on the back-burner for the sake of ministry? Are we really ready to give our lives for the Kingdom, both figuratively and literally, if need be? If the answer is no, then we must ask ourselves why. What idols are we holding fast to that are more precious than the Kingdom of our

Elohiym? And how do we overcome this? Remember Yahusha's words spoken in Matthew 16:25, *"For whoever desires to save his life will lose it, but whoever loses his life for My sake will find it."* Meditating on Messiah is essentially a means of self evaluation.

Philippians 4:8

Many of us have been taught that meditation is restricted to Scripture and, while that should be a priority, Philippians 4:8 assures us that we are not limited to that as it reads:

"Finally, brethren, whatsoever things are true, whatsoever things are honest, whatsoever things are just, whatsoever things are pure, whatsoever things are lovely, whatsoever things are of good report; if there be any virtue, and if there be any praise, think on these things."

This verse gives us permission to fill our minds with good things, that in no way de-center our Elohiym. In fact, who comes to mind when we reflect on truth, justice, purity, and so on? Who is Truth personified? Who leads us into all truth? Who came to Earth with the ultimate good report? Who is worthy of all praise?

Beyond the personhood of the Father, Son, and Holy Spirit is the fruit that they bear in the earth. We see loveliness in creation as we observe nature and a certain purity in small children. We are excited to give praise when there is good news of any kind. We see truth and justice unfold when wrongs are made right. We recognize honesty when one confesses with their mouth that they are indeed sinners in need of a Savior. We celebrate virtue when bearing witness to the character of those operating in the power of the Holy Spirit.

This can also tie in with the practice of mindful gratitude. Should we simply focus on the very first aspect of Philippians 4:1, which are things that are true, we would find a renewal of our minds taking place. Is it true that the Most High has provided you with enough food to sustain you for the day? Shelter? Transportation, even if solely by way of operative legs and feet? Is it true that He has blessed you with good health and is able to heal you of any infirmity? Is it true that He allowed you to bring children into the world and is able to open a closed womb? More importantly, is it true that the One True Living Elohiym is calling you into relationship with Him? Is it true that if you accept that call, you will no longer be the same? Is it true that you will spend eternity with your Creator? Think on these things!

<u>Implementing Meditation into other Disciplines</u>

Meditation can be a stand alone practice or it can act as an excellent companion to our other spiritual disciplines. Bible study is an obvious one, but let us even consider praise and worship. Think about when you're casually singing a song that you're familiar with versus the times when you actually let the lyrics penetrate your *leb*. How about when you're praising Yah, listing out His glorious attributes and rather than absently agreeing, while simultaneously thinking about your to-do list for later, you actually focus on what is being said, allowing it to fill you up with awe and gratefulness. These are forms of meditation which bring about a palpable difference in how we encounter the presence of the Most High. Psalms 22:3 tells us that our Elohiym inhabits the praises of His people. This requires us to be fully engaged and not just physically present.

Regarding prayer, we are told not to use vain repetitions.[143] This means we shouldn't be mindlessly repeating phrases out of habit as we work ourselves up into a frenzy and call it fervent prayer. We should be having a meaningful, passionate, and heartfelt dialog with our Heavenly Father. Practicing meditation can aid in this, along with helping us to fulfill 1 Thessalonians 5:16-18, which reads *"Rejoice evermore. Pray without ceasing. In everything give thanks: for this is the will of Elohiym in Mashiach Yahusha concerning you."* This verse is instructing us on the mindset that we are to carry throughout our day.

I spent much of my life secretly feeling overwhelmed by the idea of praying without ceasing. To my carnal mind, it seemed unrealistic and tedious. But as I grow, I see that in the midst of my day, there is always something to thank Yah for, receive clarity on, ask favor for, consider His opinion on, laugh with Him about, and of course there is always someone else that could use prayer. This requires a mind that always drifts back to Elohiym. So, to even begin praying without ceasing, we must be thinking about Him without ceasing. Understand that this is a process that develops over time. Please do not feel discouraged if it seems unattainable at the moment. This is a part of the renewing of the mind that occurs as we turn our lebs wholeheartedly back to our Creator with the aid of these spiritual disciplines.

Spiritual Warfare

No spiritual discipline will be without opposition. Yah is well aware that we cannot control every thought that enters our minds. Always several steps ahead, He gives us instructions for this in 2 Corinthians 10:5 which states, *"Casting down imaginations, and every high*

---

[143] Matthew 6:7

thing that exalts itself against the knowledge of Elohiym, and bringing into captivity every thought to the obedience of Mashiach." This means that we can immediately identify thoughts that are anti-Christ and reject them. For instance, Yah would never tell us to kill ourselves. Therefore, if we hear that, we already know the enemy is speaking and that thought should be promptly dismissed.

Once we've identified the lie, it's now time to replace it with a relevant truth. In this case, we may choose a verse such as John 10:10 where Yahusha Himself states, *"The thief does not come except to steal, and to kill, and to destroy. I have come that they may have life, and that they may have it more abundantly."* We should meditate on this and follow up with prayers to strengthen our minds against such attacking thoughts in the first place.

This is one example, but there are several prayers that we can use to fight against the attacks of the enemy. If you are like me, as one who knows what the Bible says, but falls short on where it says it, Google is your friend. I'm growing in that area but this book would not have been written in a reasonable time without it. In all things use wisdom, but know that it is okay to utilize the resources of our time to benefit us, particularly as it relates to our faith and the work we've been called to do.

Spiritual warfare may come in other forms such as suddenly feeling sleepy or other seemingly benign internal and external distractions. Be advised that one of the enemy's tactics is to wear us down so stay at it. Even if you fall short a dozen times, stay the course. Show the Most High that you are serious about diligently seeking Him and watch Him work on your behalf. Let the devil see that you have no intention of giving up and watch him flee.[144]

Practical Tips for Meditation

1. **Set-Aside Time.** Self care is the new buzzword these days, but what about soul care? The truth of the matter is we need a measure of downtime to actually process Yah's written Word, the leading of the Holy Spirit, and the ways in which He is practically working in our lives. This can seem challenging due to the busy nature of our lives. Nevertheless, as the saying goes, "we make time for what we want to make time for." This may require occasionally forgoing a favorite tv show, social media, or even casual conversations with loved ones. It is a worthy sacrifice with a high return on investment.

2. **Set the Mood.** We have spoken at length about the intricate relationship between the physical body and the *leb*. With this in mind, be sure that your environment is as free from distractions as possible and conducive to allowing your mind to focus. When time permits, I add a few drops of essential oil to my diffuser to aid my physical body in what I am attempting to accomplish spiritually. For meditation, I use Frankincense and Myrrh. Feel free to do your own research, but in short, these are herbs referenced in the Scripture that can aid with relaxation and focus. This is essentially what meditation is, quieting oneself for a greater measure of concentration.

---

[144] James 4:7

3. **Pray.** Begin by asking the Father to help you to clear your thoughts in preparation for meditation. Inform Him of your intention, be it to have greater understanding of Him, Scripture, Messiah or the renewing of your mind as stated in Philippians 4:1.

4. **Exercise Patience.** It can be extremely challenging to quiet oneself in a very noisy world so we will need to have patience with ourselves. If your mind wanders outside your scope of focus, gently bring it back, resisting the temptation to grow frustrated. As with anything, this spiritual discipline will become more fruitful with practice so be sure to extend grace to yourself. There are times when I've tried to meditate and have gotten no further than a repetitive thought or chant of the Bible verse that says, ***"Be still and know that I am Elohiym"***. We must be of the mindset that nothing is wasted with Yah, and perhaps that was all that I needed in the moment.

5. **Take Note**. You want to have something to take notes with particularly if you are meditating on Scripture. This can also be helpful if you are meditating as a stand alone process as it may bring forth revelation or more questions that you'll want to inquire with the Most High about later. If you really struggle with a wandering mind, it may be best to make a quick note about whatever unrelated topic comes up. For example, should you suddenly remember what you need to add to your grocery list, it's better to just quickly write it down to limit further distracting thoughts about forgetting.

6. **Be Open to the Leading of the Holy Spirit:** What may begin as meditation may lead to another spiritual discipline such as listening prayer, Bible study, worship, etc. It is totally

fine for the time that you spend with Yah to have an organic flow. We always want to give the Holy Spirit room to lead us rather than remain rigid in our own intentions. You may find yourself pleasantly surprised at where you end up.

A Final and Personal Word on Meditation

In the hustle and bustle of life, it is easy to count things as coincidence. Meditation positions us to receive confirmation when what we've been thinking about comes back around 2-3 times from various sources. After so many instances of this, we will begin to discern that Yah is in the midst of our thoughts. We will realize that we are no longer depending on our own intellect, nor is it coincidence, but it is indeed the Holy Spirit making sense of our ideations to lead, teach, and guide us. At its core, meditation reminds us to be mindful and present instead of just going through the motions. It inspires us to relate to our Creator with a greater measure of authenticity and intellect that He would expect of His intricately designed children.

My practice of intentional meditation is still a work in progress. While I understand the importance of it, it is not my strongest suit. Yet, the Holy Spirit is at work even in my weakness. Yah uses what little strength I do have, which sometimes doesn't equate to much more than desire, willingness, and positioning. Because He is my everything, and my very essence is found in Him, when my mind drifts, it increasingly drifts to thoughts of Him and how He's working in my life. I ponder these things, connect the dots, and sometimes Scripture comes to mind. When we have a *leb* that is set on the Most High, He will help us. Although I may not be the best at meditation *yet,* every Sabbath when I come together with my mishpacha, I am not without some form of praise and revelation.

Even more amazing, is that the revelation usually somehow coincides with what they have received during the week as well, confirming that the Holy Spirit is at work among us.

In further transparency, I was a little weary of writing on this topic due to my lack of practical application. The development of this topic from an initial blank page to its current status as one of the most extensive subjects in the book, now spanning two chapters, serves as a further example of the power of the Holy Spirit. Please let this be an encouragement to move forward in faith and patience, reminding yourself that it is not you doing the work, but instead, the power of Yah within. More importantly, He wants to do this work because He desires us. Do not allow laziness, impatience, or lack of understanding to get in the way of that. Stay the course and watch your relationship with the Most High be transformed!

CHAPTER 20

Fasting Part 1
An Overview of Biblical Fasting

"God is Spirit: and they that worship him must worship him in spirit and in truth."

— John 4:24

There is no way to appropriately worship the Most High without the indwelling of the Holy Spirit. Without the Spirit, we operate in the flesh. How can our flesh interact with the Father who is Spirit? The flesh is a mere vessel. Our mouths allow us to communicate audibly and sing praises to our Elohiym. The bones and muscles in our arms permit us to lift them in worship. Our feet take us to the places He commands us to go. Our private members and wombs are vessels used to bring forth image bearers.

All of these things must be maintained. Our mouths can only go for so long before thirst sets in. Proper food and nutrients keep our limbs prepared for the service of Elohiym. At a certain age, our internal systems alert our bodies that it's time to reproduce generating sexual desire. Therefore, the body begins to crave what is needed to keep up with the natural demands placed on it.

In His generosity, the Creator does not allow food, water, and sex to be robotic operations merely done to survive. There is pleasure associated with each of these functions which is why sometimes we eat when we're not hungry, like dessert, and married couples have sex outside of the need to procreate. There are also matters of the *leb* which are pleasing to our flesh. Having things go our way, being "successful", and receiving praise, to name a few. All of these are a part of the human experience, but when they are out of balance, they can morph into lust rendering us carnal minded. In this state, we begin to be ruled by our various *drives* whereby eating, drinking, sex, entertainment, ego, prestige, and our pursuit of material things take precedence. When this is the case, Yah's commandments become secondary, if that. Excuses about being human are made when we decide that our drives are more important than obedience to the Most High.

Fasting is the means by which we bring our carnal man into submission by denying the lusts of the flesh. When done correctly, it gets Yah's attention and He promises to be responsive to us.[145] On our end, it resets our palate, balances us, and re-orients our worldview to that of the Father's. It pleases Him to observe His intelligent creation operating in the dominion for which we were created. Animals are driven by instinct. Humans have instincts but are not to be ruled by them. The Scripture is full of calls to deny self and crucify the flesh which ultimately culminates in us presenting ourselves as a living sacrifice.

There are layers to understanding the way that flesh hinders our relationship with the Most High. I don't believe that pre-fall Adam and Eve were of the exact same constitution as current humans. My guess is that their spirit man took on more of a prominent role than their flesh as is the opposite of how we function today. Before the fall, Yah was walking in the cool of the garden with them. I won't claim to know exactly what this means beyond what it says, but from

---

[145] Isaiah 58:9

Scripture, we can observe a difference in how Yah interacted with humans post fall. There definitely seemed to be less of a face to face interaction with Yah blatantly telling Moses that no man could see His face and live, leaving Moses to observe His back. [146]

Notably, when Yah called Moses up to Mount Sinai to give him the commandments, he went without food and drink for 40 days. [147] Here, Scripture testifies to one of the first powerful manifestations of the infamous verse *"...Man shall not live by bread alone, but by every word that proceeds out of the mouth of Yahuah."*[148] During this encounter, there is a divine exchange of fleshly things for that which is holy. In this state, Moses receives the Word of Yah which instructs His people on how to love Him and one another, as a people set apart for His purposes. There is a pattern established for us here. We have the Torah that we received through Moses. We also have historical accounts, prophetic writings, and the gospels via divinely inspired men. Yet when we find ourselves needing clarity or a deeper understanding of these things, we, like Moses, can deny our flesh in pursuit of a direct word from the Most High.

Who Should Fast?

While some Believers consider fasting to be optional, it was a regular practice in Ancient Israel which did not change with the renewed covenant. In Matthew 17:20-21 Yahusha tells His disciples that though they have faith that moves mountains, certain things can only be overcome by prayer and fasting. The expectation was so great that the Pharisees criticized Yahusha's disciples by asking Him why they don't fast? He responds by saying that they do not need to

---

[146] Exodus 33:23

[147] Exodus 34:28

[148] Deuteronomy 8:3, Matthew & Luke 4:4

fast because He is with them.[149] Well, our Messiah has been gone for a very long time and it's difficult to see how anyone will be able to navigate these end times without fasting. If the deception of the last days doesn't take one out, having an undisciplined diet, particularly in the United States, will.

For those in leadership, fasting is all the more imperative. The leaders that we saw do great exploits in Scripture understood and utilized its power: Moses, King David, Queen Esther, Elijah, Daniel, Paul and even the Messiah Himself, to name a few. However, no one is exempt as we all function as leaders in some capacity be it within a faith-based organization, business, or our families. We are called to be a light to non-believers, which, though informally, denotes a form of leadership. How many times have people sought us out to pray because they know we have a connection to the Most High? While we may oblige, our intent should be to *lead* them to Him for themselves. Furthermore, there is only a certain point of spiritual growth that we can ascend to without fasting. No matter how deep we believe we have gone, we should know that if we are not denying the flesh in this way, we are inevitably falling short of our potential.

Food & Social Implications of Fasting

Food, particularly in excess, can contribute to mental and spiritual dullness. We experience it in our bodies when we consume a large meal that leaves us feeling lethargic. This is also associated with the quality of what we are eating. During a recent visit to Brazil with friends, we observed that the food quality was notably different. After dining at a Brazilian steakhouse and feasting on a variety of meats and side-dishes, we were shocked that we did not feel bogged down

---

[149] Matthew 9:14-15

and were still able to go on to enjoy the rest of the evening. If we were back home in the U.S., that meal would have been the last thing we saw before our heads hit the pillow.

Therefore, we must not only be mindful of how much we consume, but also what, remembering that our physical and spirit man are connected. It is no secret that certain additives are placed into our food supply that interfere with cognition. Fluoride in tap water and the red dye found in many junk foods, especially for children, are just a couple of examples. This is why the Daniel Fast is effective in its own right. It is basically an extreme vegan diet where food is still permitted barring meat, dairy, bread, sugar, processed foods and so forth. This gives our bodies, including our brains, a sort of reset. Some do not consider this to be a Biblical fast since it still involves eating. However, despite having done many different fasts, including dry and water for varying amounts of time, an 8 day Daniel Fast is where I received the most spiritual breakthrough to date. This type of fast could also be a good starting point for those new to the practice.

As a side note regarding tap water, while everyone may not be able to afford to drink quality bottled water, we should all be covering ourselves in prayer regarding what we eat and drink. Unless we have a farm and with our own livestock and garden, we are still at the mercy of this system whether the label says organic or not.

Another intriguing aspect of fasting is that it reveals how much of our lives are consumed with food. It's not just the eating itself. There is preparation which includes the thought process of what to eat, gathering and purchasing food, time spent cooking and clean up. Food takes up a considerable amount of our time and we would be surprised at how much of it we gain back when it is eliminated from our daily schedule.

We also tend to underestimate how much of a role food plays in our social interactions. Breaking bread is almost a part of every gathering, whether it be for religious gatherings, special occasions, courtship, or just leisurely spending time with our loved ones. To this extent, some of us may even choose to forego some of the more casual social interactions until the time of fasting is complete. Fasting is about separating ourselves unto the Most High for a period of time. Maintaining the same level of social interaction as pre-fast defeats the purpose and may also serve as a distraction. Not to mention, fasting is a private thing done between us and the Father.[150] While there is such a thing as corporate fasts and times where those in close fellowship will fast together, it is not something that we generally go around announcing.

Fasting re-aligns us to the things that are important to the Most High. It brings a stillness to our lives, putting a pause on non-essentials as we focus on spiritual matters and position ourselves to hear from Him. Many of us in the West live relatively fast paced lives, which include family dynamics, demanding careers along with recreational activities. In the midst of that, we are inundated with communal matters, political affairs, the happenings of popular culture and world news.

We can easily get lost in all of that and begin to have our perspective shaped by the world rather than our Elohiym. Fasting acts as a safeguard against this, as it is during that time that we pull away from it all to seek the voice of the Father. It is not uncommon to emerge with a different perspective on these things once a time of fasting has been completed. We also notice how much more time

---

[150] Matthew 6:16-18

we actually have for Yah when we prioritize our lives with Him rightfully at the top.

Benefits of Fasting

Physical & Mental Health

Health benefits are a by-product of fasting. It is an excellent jump start to anyone seeking to live a healthier lifestyle. If one is used to consuming large amounts of sugary, fried, or processed foods, it can feel nearly impossible to exchange these for cleaner options. There will be a much higher success rate by beginning with a palate cleanse. After drinking only water for 3 days, when our mouth finally tastes an apple or cucumber, it will be some of the best produce we've ever had. Many can testify to fasting having healed them from a variety of illnesses as well. This also speaks to fasting with the right motivations. As Believers, we do not simply fast to achieve weight loss goals. Instead, we fast to seek the Father in helping us to be more disciplined in making healthier choices while simultaneously cleansing our palate in preparation.

As alluded to earlier, food, particularly the processed fare that we consume in the U.S., can have negative effects on our brain which we use to communicate with Yah. Individuals who fast, including those who do so for reasons apart from spiritual growth, often report having increased mental clarity and improved memory. This is especially the case with extended fasts. Imagine having more time, a clearer mind to comprehend Scripture and an increased ability to hear the voice of the Holy Spirit. This is gold for a Believer seeking greater intimacy with the Most High. It is up to us to decide if temporarily abstaining from food is an important enough sacrifice to draw nearer to our Creator.

Self Control

It is commonly assumed that fasting primarily enhances self-control with respect to eating habits. Yet, fasting actually aids us in becoming more disciplined and principled overall. It helps us to realize that although we may want to do something, we don't actually have to. James 4:7 teaches us that the more we resist something, the lesser the hold it will have on us. Although this verse is specifically referencing the devil, it is also applicable to the flesh which the enemy can work through. Additionally, the first part of that Scripture tells us to ***"Submit yourselves to Elohiym."*** This infers that our resistance cannot be rooted in our willpower alone. Fasting is a form of submission to the Most High and being in His presence is what gives us the fortitude to turn away from sin and other worthless endeavors.

Self-control is not just about doing unprofitable things from time to time, but having discernment on what should be avoided altogether and having the strength to refuse. Fasting can give us enough mental clarity and spiritual power to appropriately limit, disengage, or steer clear of things that have the potential to lead us into a trap. The word *limit* is used because there are certain things that cannot be completely eliminated from our lives such as food.

Regarding food specifically, fasting literally resets our palates, particularly when done for three days or more. If we stick to the fast, we will begin to notice a difference in the types of foods we desire. If fasting for better discipline with food, it's important to include this in times of prayer as it may be an actual stronghold that may be more difficult to overcome. When done correctly, it is highly unlikely that after a system reset, our bodies would desire unnaturally sweet, processed, fried foods, etc. In fact, our bodies will lead us in what to eat and it's up to us to listen and not run to what is convenient. The power of self-control will be readily available and it's our responsibility to take advantage of it for our betterment.

It must also be said that the results will be temporary. Fasting is a weapon used to fight the ongoing battle with the flesh that will remain until our last breath. The goal is for the flesh to become increasingly weakened as we mature in our walk. In some cases, people are able to eradicate certain things from their diets for good. But for many of us, over time, we will slip back into our old ways. (Please note that I am mainly referring to unprofitable habits, not necessarily explicit sin.) At a certain point, we notice that we are leaning into our cravings too much, signaling us that it's time for another fast. This is the case with the flesh in general. If we are sensitive enough to the Spirit and self aware, we'll know when we are beginning to operate heavier in the flesh rather than the Spirit. This is the signal that it is time to consecrate ourselves *again* for a time of prayer and fasting. While this may seem extreme, if you are new to fasting, please understand that this is a regular practice for those seeking to maintain intimacy with Yah. Intentional Believers live a fasted lifestyle.

Self-Control is also a fruit of the Spirit.[151] This means the more time we spend with Yah, the greater the manifestation of the Spirit should be in us. When someone is lacking in self-control it may not always be compartmentalized to one area. Meaning, if there is lack of self control with food, there may be the same issue in other areas like financial, sexual, and even speech. Food addictions, which often lead to health issues, constant financial crisis, sexual immorality, and an unbridled tongue that continuously causes strife are all hindrances to intimacy with our Elohiym. As we discussed

---

[151] Galatians 5:23-24

earlier, instead of seeking Him about the deeper things, we become stuck addressing carnal matters because we're in constant need of rescuing. This is a form of low functioning spirituality.

Self-control is what helps us to reach for our Bibles rather than our phones. It gives us the wherewithal to turn the tv off for a while and spend that time in the Most High's presence. It aids us in realizing what's important and strengthens us to bridle our tongues instead of quarreling over trivial matters. Overall, fasting puts us on the path to alignment and brings balance to all areas of our lives. As we deny our flesh while asking Yah to search us, we are in a better position to actually see ourselves and how fruitless some of our habits truly are.

We will likely experience different outcomes after every fast, but when done correctly, we will not remain the same as we were before. Even if we don't feel as if the fast was very impactful, we must trust that Yah is always working behind the scenes on our behalf, particularly when we have chosen to deny ourselves for more of Him. Remember, we can never out give the Most High and He wastes nothing.

Breaking Addictions

Addiction sets in when the wisdom and self-control that we were trusting in fails us. Obviously, no one begins a habit with the intent to be overtaken by it to the point of compulsion. Our pride tells us that we are strong enough to not be controlled by anything. Some addictions may begin with a simple curiosity coupled with a lack of discernment and weakness. Once we experience the *reward* of what we are partaking in, it can begin to take hold of us even on a subconscious level.

The thing about addictions is that they are actually distractions that we are using to fulfill an unmet need that we may be unaware of. It is a quick fix that never truly satisfies, hence the need to keep coming back for more. Not only are we distracting ourselves from addressing the deeper issue(s) residing within us, but the amount of time, energy and resources it takes to feed the addiction is also taking away from more significant areas of our lives. It's a sick cycle that fasting can help break.

I used to have a mean Twitter addiction back in the day. The constant hits of news and information were like crack and after work I would spend hours scrolling, although I rarely posted anything. I knew that I was wasting my life, but I felt too drained to do anything about it. In hindsight, I believe the lifestyle I was living at the time, an unfulfilling 9-5, played a role in that. I also believe that it was a cycle in which I was already drained, leaving me just enough energy to scroll after work, but the scrolling itself was draining me as well. The enemy is crafty.

It took multiple fasts to break the addiction and every time I would go back I was better able to see how fruitless my time spent on the app was. I began to see how gifted individuals were giving away tons of brilliant ideas within 140 characters for the sake of a like or retweet. I also perceived how some were using the app to their advantage, meaning they were developing businesses and creative pursuits while simply using the app as a form of free advertisement. Meanwhile, I'm watching all of this instead of making strides to improve my own situation.

In summary, fasting not only enabled me to overcome the addiction, but also provided valuable insight into how the app can be beneficial when utilized appropriately. Every addict knows that there are safeguards that must remain in place when you have a particular affinity for a thing. For instance, a person who struggles with alcohol probably wouldn't keep liquor at their house. For me, it meant not using Twitter inside my home.

Fasting can loosen the stronghold of any addiction, whether it's shopping, sex, or even food itself. It is up to us to be wise in setting appropriate boundaries that keep us from backsliding. We need to have it at the forefront of our minds that no amount of sex, food, material items, etc. is more valuable than our relationship with Yah. We cannot serve two masters so we should be willing to do whatever it takes to let the lesser one go.

Fasting & Intimacy with the Most High

While this could have rightfully been at the top of the 'benefits of fasting' list, it's important to be reminded of how the other benefits, indeed, allow for more intimacy with Yah. Being mentally and physically healthy, self-controlled, and free from addiction positions us to enjoy more of Yah and what He has for us. Fasting intensifies intimacy with Yah because it makes us sensitive to His voice. This is why we should strongly consider removing as many outside distractions as possible while we fast. As I mentioned earlier, the Most High is not going to compete with anyone. He's not going to scream at us above all the noise that we are allowing during a time that is supposed to be set-apart for Him.

Fasting produces humility as we are literally depending on the Most High to see us through to the end. For some odd reason, current culture takes issue with humility. We still must understand that this characteristic is pleasing to the Most High. He says it countless times in Scripture. He even states verbatim that He resists the proud but gives grace to the humble.[152]

---

[152] James 4:6

Humility is an underrated Kingdom currency and Yah expects it to flow both vertically and horizontally. That means it is not enough to maintain a meek attitude towards Yah while displaying a prideful disposition towards our brothers and sisters. Many of us get this wrong and it is a stumbling block to our relationship with Yah. Fasting brings us to the realization that everything that we are and do is because of the grace of the Most High and has little to nothing to do with us. This understanding allows us to deal graciously with one another realizing that all that we are is because of Him![153] Yah is the one that placed every good thing in us to be used for His glory and the edification of one another. Our role is saying yes, submitting to His will and allowing ourselves to be used. This is the type of attitude that yields intimacy with the Most High.

While it may seem counterintuitive, as we are the ones denying ourselves, fasting really isn't about us. It is about Him. Yes, we go before Him with our concerns, but we leave it at His feet as we seek more of Him. This is why worship is such an integral part of fasting. It is to get our minds off of ourselves. We must even be mindful of the type of worship music that we listen to during this time. While the joy of the Most High remains in us, Biblically speaking, this is typically not a joyful time. It is a solemn time of repentance, self-reflection and seeking Elohiym in spirit and in truth. If we listen closely, we will discern that much of mainstream gospel music is very *me*-centered. This doesn't mean we can't listen to any inspirational music within the duration of the fast, particularly on an extended one. I'm simply suggesting that we be largely focused on music that is centered on reverencing Yah for who He is, regardless of what He has or will do for us. This in itself has the power to lift us up as we take our minds off of ourselves and our

---

[153] 1 Corinthians 15:10

raggedy situations, instead focusing on the glory of the Eternal Perfect One who holds all power in His hands. Ultimately, it is about humbling ourselves before Him and pouring out our adoration as we wait with expectation that He will respond to us.

Fasting also brings greater intensity to every other spiritual discipline that we employ during that period. With improved mental clarity, we can have greater focus in meditation and better comprehension while studying Scripture. It sharpens our discernment to know what and how to pray. We may even experience a greater *flow* in prayer or while prayer journaling. Fasting makes our spirit man more sensitive to Yah, allowing for a purer worship experience and a greater ability to hear Him during listening prayer. Removing the hindrances and putting significant effort into our spiritual disciplines will totally revitalize our relationship with the Most High. However, when any of these are coupled with fasting, a super serum is created with the potential to catapult us to the next level.

Through fasting, we may also receive clarity on an issue that we have been seeking Yah on for some time. It has been my experience that fasting allows Him to speak to me about the things that are important to Him. It is not uncommon that if we are fasting regarding relational issues that the Most High deals with us first before addressing the other party. Other times, the matters that He brings to light during a fast won't even be on our radar. When we submit to His will, trusting that He knows what's best for us, we would be surprised at where He may lead us. There is truly never a dull moment with the Most High. Best of all, fasting allows more room for Yah in our daily lives that we did not perceive before. More time spent with Him means greater connection to Him.

<u>Hindrances to Fasting</u>

A resistance to fasting that we can't seem to get past can be an indication of an idolatrous relationship with food. While most people aren't necessarily excited about not eating for a time, the desire for more of our Elohiym pushes us forward. As we mature in our walk, our spiritual appetites begin to outweigh our carnal ones and we look forward to the spiritual rewards of fasting. It will become a regular part of our lives as we desire for our spirit man to not only remain submitted to the Most High, but to also ascend in the spirit realm where we should be storing up treasures.

There are those who have pre-existing conditions that can make fasting challenging. This may call for the need to start small or make concessions. Yah is not going to be mad because you had some orange juice to avoid going into diabetic coma or for needing a little food to accompany prescription medicine. The fact of the matter is, we eat too much in the U.S. Even cutting out one meal a day and praying in its stead can make a difference in our spiritual lives and our physical bodies will certainly survive. Furthermore, a lot of these ailments can actually be healed by fasting; something that the healthcare system and "Big Pharma" will not want to be honest about. Nevertheless, we seek the Most High for wisdom in all things and do not allow anyone to shame us as we grow in our faith and ability to fast.

CHAPTER 21

Fasting Part 2: Practical Application

There are a variety of fasts to choose from: dry, water only, partial day, Daniel fasts and so on. The main thing to remember is that a Biblical fast will always include abstaining from food for a period of time. Today we hear people say that they are *fasting* from social media, television or secular music. While profitable, they do not meet the Biblical criteria for a fast. Fasting is meant to be a time of consecration. This means, for a set time, we withdraw from carnal pleasures with the intent of drawing nearer to the Most High and strengthening our spirit man. Therefore, disengaging from entertainment would be an expected part of the fast, but it would not constitute the fast itself. Most importantly, prayer and fasting go hand in hand. If prayer is not included in our time of fasting, then we are simply not eating.

The intentions of a fast matter. We should be leery of fasting for material things such as a new vehicle, home, or even a new job. Obviously we would pray about these things with the understanding that Yah knows what we need and will provide for us in due time. However, when it comes to fasting, it would be more appropriate to fast in preparation for what we need. Are we built up enough spiritually to deal with the pressures that come with a new position? How are we planning to reflect Mashiach on the job? Will the home that we are seeking remain an undefiled place of worship and prayer for the Spirit to comfortably inhabit? Will we be quick to use our vehicle to be a helping hand to someone in need?

As Believers, we should bear in mind that nothing we are given is meant to solely benefit ourselves. Fasting helps to de-center ourselves to see how the very blessing we are in need of can also be of use to others. We may even fast to receive wisdom from Yah on *how* to obtain what we are seeking.

A fast is not to be used as some sort of magic trick to obtain what we want. That is edging dangerously close to witchcraft and believe it or not, those who partake in dark arts do indeed fast. Again, this points to the reality of universal laws that go beyond the confines of any said religion. The very nature of depriving your carnal body automatically makes your inner man more sensitive to spiritual things. What spiritual things are being entreated is a different story.

Our Hebrew ancestors understood this and knew the power of denying their flesh for a heightened experience with their Elohiym. Biblical fasts were implemented for the sake of breakthrough, preparation, repentance, mourning, strategy, etc. We often speak of Queen Esther and Daniel's fast but there are numerous fasts in Scripture that we can reference for understanding.

What does Scripture say about fasting?

- Isaiah 58:8-9 states that proper fasting comes with promises of healing, a greater measure of righteousness, protection and accessibility to Yah.

- It is expected. Fasting has been a long-standing custom for those who have worshiped the Elohiym of Abraham, Isaac, and Jacob over the generations. This is also implied in Yahusha's instructions for fasting in Matthew 6:16-18. He begins by saying **"When you fast"** as opposed to "If you fast..." This is an expected practice for disciples of Mashiach.

- In Matthew 7:21 Yahusha says that fasting, along with prayer, is the only way for deliverance in certain situations.

- In Matthew 6:16-18, the Messiah instructs us that fasting is a private matter between us and the Father. We are not to bring attention to the fact that we are fasting. Neither should we go around looking unkempt and complaining about being hungry. Instead we are to appear normal knowing that the Father sees what is done in secret and will reward us.

- Isaiah 58:3-10 and Matthew 6:16-18 go into detail about what is considered an acceptable fast to the Most High. Isaiah 58 contains words from the Father and in Matthew 6 we have instruction from the Son. The central themes contain humility before Yah, denying our flesh, showing kindness and generosity to others, and the private nature of fasting. For your convenience, these verses in their entirety will be included at the end of the chapter. I highly suggest taking the time to read through them now and as a part of your initial fasting regime, particularly if you are new to the practice.

How to Fast: 10 Practical Tips

1. **Set Intentions.** How long is the fast? Will this be a dry, water, or a Daniel Fast? What other forms of distractions will you be abstaining from during the fast? What are you looking to accomplish? Write the answers down in your journal. You may even want to seek the Most High for direction regarding the fast. However, if you don't feel like you're getting an answer, proceed anyway. This isn't something that you can get wrong and if you do, Yah will be there to course correct.

2. **Pray Beforehand.** Ask the Most High is there anything that He would have you focus on during the fast? Also, ask Him for strength to sustain you to the end.

3. **Prepare.** Remove anything that would tempt you to break your fast. This is something that can be done a couple of days prior to your start date. You don't want to be handling a bag of chips on day one of the fast, since they could end up in your mouth on the way to the garbage can. You may decide to temporarily remove any social media apps from your phone that you may be tempted to use.

4. **Pray and Read Scripture.** These are the essentials of fasting. Prayer is how we communicate with Yah but Scripture is one of the primary ways that He speaks to us. Ask the Holy Spirit to help you perceive what Yah is saying to you and for the ability to receive revelation. Ideally, this would take place during the times you would typically eat or engage in other activities that you are temporarily abstaining from like watching TV.

5. **Worship.** This is another vital part of fasting. It is a time to glorify the Most High for the Majestic King that He is. Worship will also help to sustain you as you take your mind off your flesh and center it on Yah.

6. **Integrate other Spiritual Disciplines.** Aside from prayer and diving into Scripture, fasting is an excellent time to prayer journal, meditate, practice listening prayer, etc.

7. **Stop.** If you're fasting to break a particular habit, be sure to stop the specific behavior while fasting and cover it in prayer.

8. **Practice Generosity & Kindness.** Yah says that a fast that pleases Him includes giving to those in need. This may even

mean buying food for someone else while you yourself may be hungry. This is the type of selflessness that rises up as a sweet incense to the Most High. [154]

9. **Be Open.** Yah may not speak directly to what you are inquiring about. Instead, He may speak to you about what He wants to discuss. It may be that what you are asking is already taken care of and simply awaiting manifestation if you stay the course. Meanwhile, there may be other matters that He desires to speak to you about now that He has your undivided attention.

10. **Remember that this is a private matter.** There are times where communicating this would be necessary such as if you are fasting with someone else or among others in your household who are not fasting but are expecting you at the dinner table. When we unnecessarily tell others we are fasting, we receive the reward of man, attention, praise & adoration, rather than the priceless rewards from Yah.

A Final Note: Fasting for Repentance/Salvation

As I bring this section to a close, there is something that the Holy Spirit has laid upon my heart to include in this chapter. It was nowhere in my outline, but as I wrote, the words began to flow in this direction. In obedience to the leading of the Spirit, I want to briefly address fasting as it pertains to repentance and salvation.

When you have made the confession of repentance with your mouth, entered into the covenant through the blood of Yahusha to serve the Elohiym of the Bible, it is a good idea to fast. Sometimes we say things out of emotion, but when the challenges of life befall

---

[154] Philippians 4:16-18

us, it can be all too easy to go back on our word. ***See Matthew 13:20-22.*** I know that there are many people that subscribe to *once saved, always saved,* but I am here to tell you that this is a doctrinal lie from hell. To be fair, my own Christian upbringing fought against this for quite some time until the Most High revealed to me the error in this thinking and how it keeps so-called Believers in sin.

There are passages in both the Old and New Testament that support this, including Ezekiel 18:24 and Hebrews 10:26. Ezekiel is speaking of a physical death as a penalty for sin, but dying in your sin also means spiritual death and spending eternity apart from Yah.[155] The Scripture in Hebrews tells us straight away that there is no longer a remittance for intentional repetitive sin. I've noticed that when you bring this up, people start referencing what they have been taught or what they think it means, rather than what Scripture actually says. There are other passages that support this truth such as Galatians 5:19-21, but often no Scripture will suffice to a hardened or fearful heart.

Nevertheless, this is not a cause for despair or anxiety as we can very well be assured of our salvation. Meaning, that if we do what the Most High says, then we will spend eternity with Him. Most importantly, Yah is not out to trick us and we don't have to live in constant fear of whether or not we are going to hell. He has given us an open book test along with the Holy Spirit to ensure that we pass. It is up to us to express our free will in the careful working out of our salvation.[156] This should not be confused with *working* our way to Heaven. Rather, obedience is the demonstration of our belief, as our

---

[155] Romans 6:23
[156] Philippians 2:12

faith is proven by our works. Below, James 2:14-24 gives a practical example along with a clear teaching on this subject:

14 What does it profit, my brethren, if someone says he has faith but does not have works? Can faith save him? 15 If a brother or sister is naked and destitute of daily food, 16 and one of you says to them, "Depart in peace, be warmed and filled," but you do not give them the things which are needed for the body, what does it profit? 17 Thus also faith by itself, if it does not have works, is dead. 18 But someone will say, "You have faith, and I have works." Show me your faith without your works, and I will show you my faith by my works. 19 You believe that there is one God. You do well. Even the demons believe—and tremble! 20 But do you want to know, O foolish man, that faith without works is dead? 21 Was not Abraham our father justified by works when he offered Isaac his son on the altar? 22 Do you see that faith was working together with his works, and by works faith was made perfect? 23 And the Scripture was fulfilled which says, "Abraham believed Elohiym, and it was accounted to him for righteousness." And he was called the friend of Elohiym. 24 You see then that a man is justified by works, and not by faith only.

In summary it says, faith without works is dead but I want to address a few key points. Verse 19 says that simply believing that Elohiym exists is not sufficient. However, the Bible says that all that call upon His name shall be saved. On the other hand, the Scripture says that the Most High doesn't hear the prayers of sinners. How do we reconcile these verses? We do so with the understanding that head knowledge and lip service are not sufficient for salvation. We could liken this to a significant other that says *I love you* but continually contradicts these words with his or her actions.

Calling on His name must be done with a truly repentant heart. If we are allotted more time than the thief on the cross, whom received salvation in the final hour, then we will spend the rest of our lives proving our commitment to Yah with our works. These works include obedience to Yah's Word, Torah and Mashiach, to the best of our abilities. We also have personal assignments given to us by Yah that we accomplish by using the gifts and talents that He gave us. Lastly are the general good works that we do upon the earth such as caring for the less fortunate. The children of the Most High are known by their love demonstrated by all of the above.

These are the keys to salvation but they are never meant to be done without an authentic relationship with the Most High. In fact, it is our love for Him that drives us to do these things in the first place. Without this loving relationship, we are left with empty religion. This entire book is meant to help as many people as possible avoid falling into this trap.

There was something else that stuck out to me in James 2:20. In the verse it asks, *"**do you <u>want</u> to know that faith without works are dead?**"* In some translations it says, *"**will you know?**"* The inquiry is followed up by calling the listener *foolish* or *vain* implying a willful ignorance. It begs the question, do you really want to know your Creator or do you just want to simply be blessed and avoid going to hell? Do you really want to elevate spiritually, or do you just want to do the bare minimum to check off your boxes? Whatever the answer is, just know that Yah truly does know your heart, for better or for worse. It is also my sincere belief that He is preparing a place only for those that genuinely love Him.

As spoken of in the introduction, when I made up my mind to surrender my life to Yah wholeheartedly, I followed it up with a three day fast. When it was over, I experienced a radical change on the inside and I was never the same again. I was already at rock bottom, but I believe the fasting allowed any strongholds that would tempt me to go back on my word to be broken. When we fast for salvation, repentance will be a major part of our prayer; sincerely going before the Most High in confession, asking Him to break any strongholds, and help us to stay true to the covenant we have made with Him no matter what lies ahead. This is a holy prayer that the Most High will honor if we do so genuinely.

I sincerely hope that this chapter has served as an informative and motivational resource to make fasting a priority in your spiritual walk. It is a personification of presenting ourselves as living sacrifices as we sacrifice our flesh which is perishing by the moment, for the perfecting of our spirit man which is eternal. We do so in preparation to spend eternity with One Who was, Who is, and Who will always be.

Isaiah 58:3-10

3. *"Why have we fasted, they say, 'and You have not seen? Why have we afflicted our souls, and You take no notice?' In fact, in the day of your fast you find pleasure, And exploit all your laborers."*

4. *"Indeed you fast for strife and debate, And to strike with the fist of wickedness. You will not fast as you do this day, To make your voice heard on high."*

5. *"Is it a fast that I have chosen, A day for a man to afflict his soul? Is it to bow down his head like a bulrush, And to spread out sackcloth and ashes? Would you call this a fast, an acceptable day to Yahuah?"*

6. *"Is this not the fast that I have chosen: To loose the bonds of wickedness, To undo the heavy burdens, To let the oppressed go free, And that you break every yoke?"*

7. *"Is it not to share your bread with the hungry, And that you bring to your house the poor who are cast out; When you see the naked, that you cover him, And not hide yourself from your own flesh?"*

8. *"Then your light shall break forth like the morning, Your healing shall spring forth speedily, And your righteousness shall go before you; The glory of Yahuah shall be your rear guard."*

9. *"Then you shall call, and the Lord will answer; You shall cry, and He will say, 'Here I am.' If you take away the yoke from your midst, The pointing of the finger, and speaking wickedness,"*

10. *"If you extend your soul to the hungry And satisfy the afflicted soul, Then your light shall dawn in the darkness, And your darkness shall be as the noonday."*

Matthew 6:16-18

16. *"When you fast, do not look somber as the hypocrites do, for they disfigure their faces to show others they are fasting. Truly I tell you, they have received their reward in full."*

17. *"But when you fast, put oil on your head and wash your face,"*

18. *"So that it will not be obvious to others that you are fasting, but only to your Father, who is unseen; and your Father, who sees what is done in secret, will reward you."*

CHAPTER 22

Community

This writing largely focuses on the individual's path to intimacy with the Creator. Nevertheless, I would be remiss not to include the importance of community as Yah cultivates intimacy through this means as well. Similar to an earthly parent, the Most High enjoys being in the midst of His children gathered together. After all, the original idea was for His people to live righteously and peacefully among one another as they glorified the One True Living Elohiym before the watching nations.

Today, as the Messiah has opened the door for both natural and grafted in branches, it is no secret that we all belong to the body of Mashiach. 1 Corinthians 12:12-31 goes to great lengths to describe how regardless of our background and status, our individual gifts and roles are meant to edify one another and bring glory to our King as a cohesive unit. Through community we are able to witness and confirm the moving of the Holy Spirit in ways that we may be unable to detect alone. There is also a measure of safety and blessing in community along with elements of growth that can only be attained within the context of other Believers.

Therefore, allow me to be clear: having a faith-based community is essential. While it is not absolutely necessary to attend a church, the Scriptures tell us not to forsake the assembling of the saints. [157] This is an important distinction because there was a time where one could feel confident in easily finding a *Bible believing*

---

[157] Hebrews 10:25

church after placing their trust in the Messiah. Unfortunately, times have changed. As lawlessness, deception, and the separation between wheat and tares persist, joining a church or assembly should be done with prayer, patience, and confirmation.

What's important is to have at least one other person that we are walking in spiritual agreement with. This person should be able to pray with and for us, discuss the Word, provide Biblical based counsel, encouragement, and hold us accountable. While there is an individual aspect to our relationship with Yah, there are levels of intimacy that are found in the midst of gathering Believers. He says, ***"For where two or three are gathered together in my name, there am I in the midst of them."***[158]

Seasons of Consecration

There are times when a Believer may need to step away from the masses to seek Yah for his or herself apart from the noise. I have seen countless testimonies where people plead with the Most High to reveal Himself to them in a way that they can truly recognize and understand. That can be hard to receive while surrounded by so many others imposing their image of Him onto us. It is during the process of stepping away that the disciplines mentioned in this book are paramount. If we step away without Scripture and foundational beliefs, we're left vulnerable to the enemy's tactics that can be heightened by isolation.

During times of solitude or even within a very small community, it's important to perceive the significance of the season and the work that Yah is doing in us. We may be experiencing a time of unlearning and relearning that the Most High does not want tainted

---

[158] Matthew 18:20

by the traditions of man.[159] In the beginning of my season of seclusion, I repeatedly asked Yah to send me a mentor. He initially refused, but after much persistence, He gave me what I asked for. After a few interactions with these individuals, and a couple of attempts at becoming a part of a community, I realized why He said no in the first place.

From those experiences, I learned to be content, while remaining focused on Him and obedient. In due time, He supernaturally sent me a like-minded sister in the faith who I was able to grow with. It was more of a mutual mentorship which Yah used to expedite my spiritual growth tremendously. It made my brief time of solitude and the closed doors to a larger community make sense. While we both had a measure of online fellowship with a couple of women assemblies, it was just the two of us on a day to day basis. After much inner work for us both, we are starting to sense that Yah is moving us to be able to congregate with more like-minded sisters. We do so at the leading of the Holy Spirit which allows us to move in wisdom and according to His perfect timing.

It is important to realize when your chapter of seclusion has ended. It can be easy to become comfortable in that season which can lead to isolation. When we isolate ourselves, we don't have to deal with other people's spiritual hang-ups, varying interpretations, and personality quirks. However, that attitude is not conducive to the type of maturity that the Most High wants to produce in us. Bearing with one another in patience, resolving conflict in love, and reasoning with each other over Scripture refines us. It is also a way to test if the fruit of the Spirit is actually operating within.

---

[159] Colossians 2:8

Outside of those struggling with trauma and self love, it is typically fairly easy to be patient, kind, and loving to ourselves. Ironically, we are always in agreement with *me, myself, and I* so there is little conflict to be resolved. Similar to marriage, community holds up a mirror so we can see ourselves and metaphorically fix our hair before our Bridegroom arrives!

Re-emerging from a Season of Seclusion

We should be mindful that these seasons are temporary and preparatory for reintegration into the body of like-minded Believers at some point. It is also important to have a solid foundation before we join another community. I would even consider it a matter of spiritual safety considering the times and state of the faith. Having a firm foundation builds up confidence to stand our ground in what we know to be true, based on Yah's Word. Therefore, when we experience situations that are anti-Christ, we have the courage to speak truth in hopes of repentance or even remove ourselves altogether if necessary.

As the time nears for us to return to a measure of fellowship, there are some things to bear in mind. With the lure of big personality pastors, exquisite buildings and large, *thriving* communities where one is all but assured of friendship and courtship, it's important to ask the following question: Will they usher you through the narrow gate that Messiah tells us we must enter the Kingdom through?[160] It is easy to get caught up in all of the other things and lose sight of your First Love in the process. [161]

In fact, I've been studying the churches mentioned in Revelation 2 and 3. Originally, I was taught that each of these

---

[160] Matthew 7:13-14

[161] Revelation 2:4

churches represented a specific church age and that we were currently in the Laodicean age whereby most people are lukewarm. While this is true, evidence of the other churches are just as prevalent; corrupt, compromised, dead, and loveless. We may have to look a little further overseas where human rights are less liberal, but should we do so, we will surely find the persecuted church. Along with warnings, these chapters are essentially messages to the *called out* Believers of all generations to be on the lookout for a community similar to the one described as Philadelphia. A rare jewel in today's time.

When we feel the gentle pull of the Holy Spirit leading us to connect with another Believer or community, it is important not to resist. Of course this should be done with caution through prayer and even fasting if needed. However, community is very important to Yah so He will make His desires clearly known if this is how He is leading you. Below, I've provided a few helpful tips for re-integrating into a faith-based community.

- **Differentiate** between your intimate circle and your extended family of Believers. Within larger groups, there is bound to be differences in how people view the Scripture and apply it to their lives. While we would want to stay clear of any anti-Christ beliefs or doctrines of devils, it's important to allow others to serve their Elohiym how they see fit.[162] Equally important is not to take on the burdens of other people's convictions. For instance, there are some who believe that it is wrong for women to wear pants. The Scripture never says this. It says that women should not dress as men and men should not wear women's attire. In our

---

[162] Romans 14:4

current culture, pants are made for women and it doesn't necessarily take away from the feminine appearance in which Yah shaped them. Still, for some people, it is a strong conviction and there is no telling them otherwise. If such people cannot co-exist without projecting their own questionable convictions onto us, then they may need to be someone that remains a part of our extended family of Believers to avoid unnecessary strife. While there may be some differences even among the inner circle, we navigate this by maintaining a mature attitude, rather than a legalistic one that attempts to force someone else into our image.

- **Be open and receiving.** When you have been led by Yah to a community of Believers, He has sent you there to both give and receive. This doesn't mean you have to take everything that is said as gospel. At the very least, be willing to take it back to the Holy Spirit for confirmation. I've seen people block or delay their progress because Yah sent a message through a particular person, but, because of who the messenger was, it wasn't received. This also ties into humility in that we should be willing to learn from our brothers and sisters whether they be elders or new to the faith. Yah is never limited in His choices on who to use.

- **Resist the urge to quarrel.** It amazes me how those who claim to keep the commandments of Yah often overlook what the Scripture says about quarreling. There are two key verses that speak directly to this:

  o 2 Timothy 2:23-25: "Don't have anything to do with foolish and stupid arguments, because you know they produce quarrels. 24 And the Lord's servant must not be quarrelsome but must be kind to everyone, able to teach,

> not resentful. 25 Opponents must be gently instructed, in the hope that God will grant them repentance leading them to a knowledge of the truth;"

- o Philippians 2:14-15: "Do all things without murmurings and disputings: 15 That ye may be blameless and harmless, the sons of Elohiym, without rebuke, in the midst of a crooked and perverse nation, among whom ye shine as lights in the world."

These verses bring up two significant areas of instruction. First, we should not be arguing to begin with. If we sense that someone has a contentious spirit, we may prayerfully consider confronting the person, in a loving manner, as an effort to bring about peace. Should that not work, then we are given permission to distance ourselves from those who are prone to quarreling. This does not mean that there will not be disagreements, but the Scripture gives numerous instructions on how to communicate with one another. If we seek these out and embody them, we will be able to speak our piece and leave the rest to the Righteous Judge.

- **Remain firm in what you know.** This requires discernment, particularly in light of the point about being open. It is a delicate balance that requires us to have an active relationship with the Holy Spirit. We have to be able to distinguish between when what we know is true or when we are experiencing cognitive dissonance. Meaning, that we are being made uncomfortable about a revelation that conflicts with what we think we already know. We can look to my experience with the *once saved always saved* doctrine as an example. Nevertheless, as your relationship with the Most

High progresses, there are going to be points of no return where you know that you know what you know. People may not always understand, but if we know Yah has spoken to us about something, then we have to stand on faith regardless of what people are saying. This doesn't always mean that we have to defend it. It may be for us to hide it in our hearts, leaving Yah to affirm it or quite possibly correct or further our understanding on the matter without human interference. We can look to Miryam, the mother of Yahusha, as an example. She knew that an angel had visited her to tell her that she would give birth to the Messiah. While others had much commentary on the topic, she kept quiet, pondering the matter in her heart. [163]

- **Keep silent.** As an addendum to the point above, a part of building intimacy with Yah is maintaining a level of privacy, even within community. I didn't understand this in my introductory years into the prophetic. I was so happy to be hearing from Yah that I would naively tell anyone who would listen. While there is a corporate component to our faith which involves sharing what we've learned, confessing our faults, praise reports, etc., there is also a private aspect. As with any relationship, some things will stay between us and the Most High unless or until He gives us permission to share. Additionally, we may not have the full understanding on some issues and risk bringing confusion by speaking on them prematurely.

- **Focus on *being* rather than *announcing*.** This goes hand in hand with being quick to hear and slow to speak, a concept that in some form or another, is repeated

---

[163] Luke 2:17-19

throughout Scripture. We have the ability to overwhelm, confuse, and intimidate people with our words. Instead, we want to strive to simply walk our faith out, expressing curiosity in others with hopes of it being reciprocated. This gives us the opportunity to share according to how the Holy Spirit is leading us. Proverbs 10:19 states, ***"In the multitude of words sin is not lacking, But he who restrains his lips is wise."*** This means if we keep talking, eventually, we're going to do one of the following: lie, exaggerate, overshare, gossip, offend, intimidate, or bring confusion. Furthermore, a lot of Believers tend to establish an identity based on what they *don't* do instead of one rooted in Messiah, who did a lot![164] In community, it's important to build on the things that we have in common and let the rest of our walk speak for itself.

- **Do not compare yourself to other Believers.** We are all at varying places on our way to the same destination. Each of us have been gifted with a way to edify the Body of Mashiach and we need not covet the gifts of others. Instead, we should be relishing in the fact that Yah has created us exactly to His preferred specifications. Our disposition should be one of gratitude for the 1 or 5 talents that we have while utilizing them for the glory of our Creator.

- **Remember that we are all broken vessels.** It doesn't matter if it's the pastor, teacher, prophet, evangelist, or apostle. All of us see in part, and while we should give honor where honor is due, everyone must be held accountable. If a word doesn't sit right with us, as in it doesn't quite line up with Scripture, we need to seek Yah in prayer for understanding. Most importantly, we should only be following leaders as

---

[164] John 21:25

they follow the Most High, being careful not to idolize any man.

- **Remain rooted in Mashiach alone.** In the Christian faith, it was be frowned upon to be what is called a church hopper. There is some validity to this in terms of one who flees at the first sign of conflict or cavalierly goes from place to place in search of some type of utopian community. Nonetheless, when we put aside man's religious ideals and shortcomings, and actually return to what is Biblical, we will see something different. Our Hebrew ancestors were sojourners, for various reasons, as it was never their custom to stay in one place permanently. We see constant examples of Yah commanding His servants to leave one place for another and sending His people on various missions. Even during the time of Mashiach, there was a lot of moving around to spread the gospel. Point being, it is essential that we remain sensitive to when the Holy Spirit is actually leading us to move on. If we are not careful, too much time in the same place with the same people can breed stagnation and complacency. Although we may love our brothers and sisters dearly, we must not hold on to anyone or anything tighter than our Elohiym and the purposes that He has for our lives. As we remain focused on our earthly assignments, we can be comforted in the fact that in due time, we will reunite with our loved ones in Mashiach and spend eternity with them.

My hope is that whether you are in or between communities, that you will remember that you are never alone. Yah is aware of our communal needs. He also knows that our greatest need is Him. As Believers, we should make it our goal to grow in appreciation of the companionship of our Creator. There is truly nothing like it and it produces a liberating contentment that shields us from unhealthy co-dependency on others. As we patiently allow Him to do the inner work that is needed in us, not only will we grow in love and intimacy with Him, but we will also become better versions of ourselves that are fit and safe for our brothers and sisters to be in community with.

CHAPTER 23

Practical Ways to Overall Intimacy with the Most High

Spiritual disciplines are essential for any Believer to mature and obtain the closeness to our Elohiym that we desire. Here are a few more practices that I believe can be helpful in our pursuit of greater intimacy with the Father.

Self-Assess

To begin, it's important for us to do an honest assessment of where we are. Self examination is a biblical principle that 2 Corinthians 13:5, along with several other passages of Scripture, instruct us to take part in. The following questions can provide greater clarity on how we see Yah and where we stand in our walk with Him. These four questions touch on 4 key areas of our spiritual walk: Belief, Trust, Obedience, and Fruit, which should be a natural by-product of the former three.

1. Do you really believe in the Elohiym of the Bible? Do you truly believe He exists?

2. Do you believe Yah beyond head knowledge that He exists? Do you believe what He has revealed about Himself; that He is good, just, and has your best interest in mind?

3. Are you obedient to His Word? If not, what is hindering you from obeying Him?

4. What fruit are you producing for the Kingdom? Note: this is not the same as personal success. How are you using your gifts to glorify Yah and serve others? What about you and your life would identify you to onlookers as a set-apart servant of the Most High?

As you ponder your answers, it is important to be honest but be careful not to fall into condemnation. This is not meant to incite guilt or shame. It is to provide a general understanding of where you are in your faith so that with the help of the Holy Spirit, you can create a new path forward to spiritual growth.

Document Your Journey

The frailty of human memory has been repeatedly highlighted throughout Scripture. It is important to keep track of all that Yah has done for you along with the milestones of your spiritual growth. This helps you to have an accurate account so that you are able to see things soberly. It also guards against the enemy's ability to deceive you, telling you lies about both yourself and the Most High. It's hard to tell someone that they have not accomplished anything when there is a written record of it right in front of their face, or that their Elohiym doesn't love them when you have an entire list of answered prayers, deliverance, blessings, and breakthroughs. Here are some practical ways to keep record:

1. Journaling. While beneficial, it doesn't have to be daily.

2. Answered prayer list for both yourself and those you have prayed for.

3. Gratitude list.

The last two don't necessarily have to be separate lists as they may be covered in your journal entries. Just be sure that there is a record of it somewhere.

The Name of Yah

As I mentioned towards the beginning of the book, we have truly been divorced from the foundations of our faith which include the use of Yah's covenant name. The Word repeatedly tells us that there is power in His name. We know that *God* and *Lord* are not names but titles. As a reminder, the name Jesus is a Greek name, not the Hebraic name He was given by the angel of the Most High.[165] My intent is not to debate whether or not the name Jesus has power or not, as I believe that it does. Yah knows that His people have been hoodwinked and bamboozled by Greek culture and that Jesus was simply the name passed down to us. But as we come into a greater measure of understanding, what is preventing us from moving forward in truth? There is something endearing about being called by our various roles such as mommy and daddy. This is why the Scripture says that as children of Elohiym, our spirits cry out to Him as *Abba*.[166] At times, my loved ones and I refer to each other as friend, sister, cousin, etc. Yet, there is something special about being called by our actual name that tends to get our attention. How much more so for the One who tells us to call upon His holy Name?

I understand that this may be uncomfortable at first. It's sad that other Believers act like you're in a cult when you actually do what the Bible instructs. However, as you grow in intimacy with the Most High, the power of other people's opinions will lessen. You will eventually realize that they are the ones on the broad path while

---

[165] Luke 1:31

[166] Romans 8:15

you, yourself, grow in confidence in living for an audience of one. Until then, I would suggest that you start by simply using a covenant name for Him during your private time.

I'm also not going to get hung up on a specific name because there are several Hebraic versions that are frequently used. Some call the Father *Ahaya, Yahuah, or Yahweh*. Common names for the Messiah include Yeshua, Yashayah, or Yahusha. Yah has many names and ways that He has revealed Himself over time. Before Moses, the Most High was often referred to as El Shaddai, The Almighty. When Moses asked, who should He tell the people sent Him, Yah replied, "I am that I am" (Ahaya) sent you. Meanwhile, the name *Yahuah* was given to be used as a memorial of the exodus from Egypt. As we await the second deliverance and gathering of Yah's true people[167], I believe this is why this particular name has resurfaced. Feel free to do a little research of your own to see how you are led but do not get stuck in analysis paralysis. In due time, Yah will bring His people onto one accord with how He wishes to be addressed. In the meantime, we inch forward in truth the best way we can. So begin calling on the actual name of Yah and allow it to add an extra layer of intimacy and power to your private time with Him.

Devotion to Truth

As I've mentioned several times, the Truth is a Person. The Scripture says that there is no shadow or turning in the Father.[168] No lie can exist in Him or His presence. This means we must be committed to truth no matter how uncomfortable it may be. We cannot have intimacy with the Most High without it. This does not

---

[167] Isaiah 11:11, Jeremiah 30:3, Ezekiel 37:21, Zechariah 8:7-8,
[168] James 1:17

mean we are on a constant quest for new information and unearthing hidden mysteries. Many of us do this thinking that we are pursuing Yah when we are actually pursuing knowledge that never really amounts to much.[169] It's reminiscent of *itching ears* surmounting in a form of self-righteousness as we find new things that we should or should not be doing. More often than not, these things are not specified anywhere in the Bible.

To be clear, the Scripture says that we should obtain knowledge lest we perish without it. But the source of this knowledge is Yah Himself as it states in Proverbs 2:6 ***"For Yahuah gives wisdom: out of his mouth comes knowledge of Elohiym."*** This means that we are to let the Holy Spirit lead us to the knowledge that we need at a specific time. I am not against doing research to increase our understanding, but I would encourage us to practice being led to read certain materials rather than just absorbing any and everything. Doing so runs the risk of consuming *meat* that is too strong for us which may lead to confusion and distraction.

When He does lead us into greater understanding, we should not harden ourselves against it when it does not coincide with our religious traditions or doctrines of man. We must be committed to the truth if we are going to remain and grow in His presence. If we continue to move in deception once truth has been revealed, we will soon reach an impasse because, again, lies cannot dwell within the presence of the Most High. Are we going to cling to what we thought we knew or are we going to cling to Yah? Intimacy with the Most High means trusting Him to lead us. He knows where we are, what we can handle, and what will profit us for the assignment(s) that He has for each of our lives.

---

[169] 2 Timothy 3:7

The Role of Grace

Remember the role of grace in all of this. As Yah has extended more grace to us than any of us rightfully deserve, we need to be sure to view ourselves through the same lens. I believe I've made it clear in this book that we are not to abuse grace. We have to realize that as Believers, we are being prepared to spend eternity with the perfect Father in His perfect Kingdom. That is not something to be taken lightly nor is it something that will happen overnight. This life is the training field so to speak, and while we may experience some radical changes during conversion, the remainder of our life will be spent being molded unto perfection.

Therefore, I humbly plead with anyone reading this, to not let satan stifle your growth with condemnation, unworthiness, or comparison to others. If you weren't worthy, Yah wouldn't be inviting you to commune with Him. If He wasn't willing to see you through to the end of your race, He wouldn't call you. Most importantly, He has distinctively made you as a one of a kind original, designed to reflect His glory in only the unique way that you can. The end goal is to bring you to perfection through an intimate life with Him.

I truly hope this book has generated an excitement within you about having a relationship with the Creator of the universe that is beyond what you thought was possible. It is a journey that will be met with challenges, but just as with the Hebrew boys, He promises to stand in the fire beside us. The reward for inviting Him in is a life of abundance on this side and rewards untold in eternity.

"But as it is written, Eye has not seen, nor ear heard, neither have entered into the heart of man, the things which Elohiym has prepared for them that love Him." — 1 Corinthians 2:9

In this hour, Yah is calling for His chosen elect to shed off the dead weight of sin, worldliness, and religion. He is beckoning us to come out from among them and be separate. He is directing us to the narrow path[170] that, alone, leads to Him. Will you accept the call? The call to have your *leb* renewed and be given the mind of Mashiach. Mashiach, the Anointed One, who was with the Father before He was with us. Mashiach who, because He was so intimately acquainted with the presence of Yah, had a mind that stayed focused on Him. Let it be so for all of us that seek to follow His example and know the Father as He did.

---

[170] Matthew 7:13-14, Luke 13:23-24

Conclusion

The Love Languages of Yah

Did you know that the Father is fluent in all 5 love languages?[171]

Words of Affirmation - The entire Bible is a letter filled with declarations of love.

Acts of Service - Yah came to Earth, in the person of Yahusha to save us. "I came to serve and not be served." - Yahusha HaMashiach

Physical Touch - The Most High is a healer and He is certainly capable of making His presence known. Many of His children testify to experiencing physical embraces from Him.

Quality Time - He desires to fellowship with us. He promises to always be with us.

Gifts - He is the gift. He rightfully boasts about giving good gifts.

Yah models love in its truest form so that we might recognize what it actually looks like. It's not the all-permissive, one-sided, sugar-coated version many of us were taught. It is a holy love, rooted in honor, boundaries, accountability, clear expectations, and reciprocity. Through His example, we learn not only how to give and receive love, but also how to discern when we have been settling for less.

May we allow His love to redefine us, stretch us, and call us higher, until we love as He does. Love isn't just what He gives, it is

---

[171] *Chapman, Gary. The 5 Love Languages: The Secret to Love That Lasts. Northfield Publishing, 1992.*

who He is. I invite you to sit with this truth, not just in thought, but in prayer, reflection, and pursuit. Let it lead you deeper into *intimacy*, beyond religion, with the One who loved you first.

"Beloved, let us love one another: for love is of Elohiym, and everyone who loves has been born of Elohiym, and knows Elohiym. He that loves not knows not Elohiym: for Elohiym is love. In this was manifested the love of Elohiym toward us, because that Elohiym sent his yachiyd[172] into the world, that we might live through him. Herein is love, not that we loved Elohiym, but that he loved us, and sent his Son to be the appropriation for our sins. Beloved, if Elohiym so loved us, we also ought to love one another." —1 John 4:7-11

---

[172] Beloved Son

Acknowledgements

All praises to the Most High, King of Glory, El Shaddai, Ancient of Days, Adonai Tzeva'oth, Yahuah Rophe'ka! Hear O' Yasharel, Your Elohim is one with many names reflecting His immaculacy! All power, glory and honor to the name above all names, the risen Yahusha Ha'Maschiach! We await Your return, Lion of Judah!

I find myself both humbled and excited that You have chosen me as a vessel to bring forth this work. Father, You are truly everything to me, and as I tell you regularly, I love my life with You. You are more than I deserve and I am so very grateful to be Yours.

To my mother, Ms. Deborah Campbell, thank you for planting a seed of faith in me as a young child. Because of you, I have no recollection of what it is like to live life without an acute awareness of my Creator. Thank you for being the best friend that I have ever had and a shining example of kindness, humility, and selfless-ness that I continuously strive to emulate.

If anyone has heard me talk about my faith for more than 5 minutes, I inevitably make mention of someone who I typically refer to simply as my prayer partner. Consheda Ashley, I have never been so intimately acquainted with someone who shares the same passion for the Father as I do. The fact that we are as different as night and day is a testament to Yah's mysterious ways and sense of humor. Nevertheless, this book would not have been what it is apart from your influence and powerful intercessory prayers. Thank you for your selflessness and commitment to your post. Most of all, thank you for being you, sis.

Also, a special thank you to everyone who responded to the survey I sent out back in 2021. The questionnaire was a part of the research I was conducting for a book initially entitled "Letters to Our Elders." At the time I was attempting to explore the growing disconnect from the faith, which from my perspective, appeared to be generational. I truly appreciate the transparency and candor with which you all shared your childhood to present day experiences of faith with me. While there was a change of plans in terms of the actual project, please know that your input was still of immense value to the composition of Beyond Religion.

The Most High has blessed me with a tremendous network of loved ones. In some way, each of you have contributed to me being the me that was able to be used to write this book. So from the bottom of my heart I would like to take this moment to extend a sincere thank you to each of you…simply for loving me, laughing with me, being patient with me, taking care of me, covering me, praying for me, paying for me…literally for every kind gesture which, to me, feels infinite. I love you. May the very best of Yah's blessings be upon you and yours forever.